Praise for
Books from The Planning Shop

"User-friendly and exhaustive … highly recommended. Abrams' book works because she tirelessly researched the subject. Most how-to books on entrepreneurship aren't worth a dime; among the thousands of small business titles, Abrams' [is an] exception."

—*Forbes*

"There are plenty of decent business-plan guides out there, but Abrams' was a cut above the others I saw. *The Successful Business Plan* won points with me because it was thorough and well organized, with handy worksheets and good quotes. Also, Abrams does a better job than most at explaining the business plan as a planning tool rather than a formulaic exercise. Well done."

—*Inc.*

"This book stands head and shoulders above all other business plan books, and is the perfect choice for the beginner and the experienced business professional. Rhonda Abrams turns writing a professional, effective business plan into a journey of discovery about your business."

—*BizCountry*

"If you'd like something that goes beyond the mere construction of your plan and is more fun to use, try *The Successful Business Plan: Secrets & Strategies* by Rhonda Abrams … This book can take the pain out of the process."

—*Small Business School (PBS television show)*

"As a small business advisor, I use the Electronic Financial Worksheet (EFW) tool extensively in analyzing my clients' financials. I recommend the Planning Shop's EFW for any small business. It's the best cash flow financial planning tool on the market today."

—*Joe Lam, Certified Business Advisor, Texas State University Small Business Development Center*

"At last, a straightforward book that demystifies the process behind conducting effective business research. *Successful Business Research: Straight to the Numbers You Need—Fast!* gives business practitioners and students an incredibly useful tool to enable them to find accurate and timely information for business plans, academic papers, and other business uses."

—*Molly Lavik, Practitioner Faculty of Marketing, Graziadio School of Business and Management, Pepperdine University*

Need to Find an Investor Fast?
This book is for you!

Are you looking for money to start or expand your business? Do you wonder how to locate someone with the funds to help you achieve your dreams? Do you want to learn how to make the kind of pitch that will cause potential investors to whip out their checkbooks? Then this book is for you!

There's an amazing amount of money being poured into smaller and newer companies by angel investors. Angel investors are individuals who invest their own money in companies—most frequently start-up businesses.

Angel financing has been expanding at an amazing rate, and there's a huge amount of angel money out there for new and growing businesses. There are literally *billions* of dollars being invested every year. For instance, over $23 billion was invested by angels in 2005. And that's just the money that's tracked by professional angel investment research!

The number of angel groups has also been growing rapidly. Virtually every large and mid-size community in America now has at least one group of angel investors. It's easier now than ever before to find and attract an angel investor—if you know how. That's where this book comes in.

Finding an Angel Investor In A Day was created for busy people like you. This guide provides you with the critical information you need, including:

- How and where to locate an individual angel investor

- How to find angel groups

- How to prepare yourself and your company for the angel investment process

- How to make the kind of pitch that convinces angels yours is an opportunity they won't want to miss

- The key terms and concepts you'll discuss with potential funders, including the all-important term sheet

- Insight into how to improve your negotiating position with investors, resulting in better valuation for your company and a better deal for you!

Finding an Angel Investor In A Day provides you with the information and insight you need to find and convince an angel investor to fund your business. And it helps you get *it done right, get it done fast!*

Finding an Angel Investor In A Day

Get it done right, get it done fast™

The Planning Shop
and **Joseph R. Bell**
with **Tracey Taylor**

Foreword by Kinko's founder
Paul Orfalea, author of *Copy This!*

the**Planning**shop

PALO ALTO, CALIFORNIA

Finding an Angel Investor In A Day: Get it done right, get it done fast!™
©2007 by Rhonda Abrams. Published by The Planning Shop™

ISBN 13: 978-0-9740801-8-5
ISBN: 0-9740801-8-7
PCN: 2006935592

Managing Editor: Maggie Canon
Project Editor: Mireille Majoor
Cover and interior design: Diana Van Winkle, Arthur Wait

Services for our readers

Colleges, business schools, corporate purchasing:
The Planning Shop offers special discounts and supplemental materials for universities, business schools, and corporate training. Contact:

> info@PlanningShop.com
> or call 650-289-9120

Free business tips and information:
To receive The Planning Shop's free email newsletter on starting and growing a successful business, sign up at: *www.PlanningShop.com.*

> The Planning Shop™
> 555 Bryant Street, #180
> Palo Alto, CA 94301 USA
> 650-289-9120
>
> Fax: 650-289-9125
> Email: info@PlanningShop.com
> *www.PlanningShop.com*

The Planning Shop™ is a division of Rhonda, Inc., a California corporation.

Printed in Canada

10 9 8 7 6 5 4 3 2

The *In A Day* Promise
Get it done right, get it done fast

You're busy. We can help.

The Planning Shop is dedicated to helping entrepreneurs create and grow successful businesses. As entrepreneurs ourselves, we understand the many demands placed on you. We don't assume that you're a dummy, just that you're short on time.

This *In A Day* book will enable you to complete a critical business task in a hurry—and in the right way. We'll guide you through the process, show you what you absolutely have to do, and give you tips and tricks to help you reach your goals.

We've talked to the experts and done the research so you don't have to. We've also eliminated any unnecessary steps so you don't waste your valuable time. That's the *In A Day* promise.

Can you find an angel investor in just one day? Well, in less than a day, with the help of this book, you can learn what you need to know to locate an angel, develop a plan of action to find the right investor for you, grasp the terms you need to know to be comfortable talking with potential funders, and then discover how to best pitch to an angel and begin negotiations.

When you have a business task you need to do now, The Planning Shop's *In A Day* books will help you get it done—in as little as a day. You'll *get it done right, and get it done fast!*

About
Joseph R. Bell

Joseph R. Bell is an Associate Professor of Entrepreneurship at the University of Arkansas at Little Rock and the CEO of Bell Consulting, LLC, a 13-member business-advisement firm. Joe has an MBA in Finance from Michigan State University and a Law degree from Thomas M. Cooley Law School.

Joe began his career as a securities attorney syndicating real estate projects, and oversaw more than $1 billion of IPOs representing 150 offerings annually. He served as director of two small business centers and went on to the Governor's Office to direct Colorado's statewide small business program. He then became the executive director of the Bard Center for Entrepreneurship Development at the University of Colorado, where he managed the Rutt Bridges Venture Capital Fund, as well as the school's new-business incubator.

While an assistant professor and director of the Entrepreneurship Center at Monfort College of Business (winner of the 2004 Malcolm Baldrige National Quality Award) at the University of Northern Colorado, Joe was concurrently the COO for CTEK Angels, where he reviewed new deals and worked with entrepreneurs to prepare their presentations to the seventy-five-member angel investor network.

His academic research and publications on angel investing have garnered national awards, including the 2006 U.S. Association for Small Business and Entrepreneurship/Small Business Institute's "Best Workshop/Symposia Small Business Award" and the McGraw-Hill/Irwin Outstanding Paper Award for "Educating Entrepreneurs on Angel and Venture Capital Financing Options," of which he was co-author.

About
The Planning Shop

The Planning Shop specializes in creating business resources for entrepreneurs. The Planning Shop's books and other products are based on years of real-world experience, and they share secrets and strategies from entrepreneurs, CEOs, investors, lenders, and seasoned business experts. Entrepreneurs have used The Planning Shop's products to launch, run, and expand businesses in every industry.

CEO Rhonda Abrams founded The Planning Shop in 1999. An experienced entrepreneur, Rhonda has started three successful companies. Her background gives her a real-life understanding of the challenges facing people who set up and run their own businesses. The author of numerous books on entrepreneurship, Rhonda has had three books appear on Bookscan's Top 50 Business Bestseller list. Her first book, *The Successful Business Plan: Secrets & Strategies,* has sold over 600,000 copies and was acclaimed by *Forbes* and *Inc.* magazines as one of the top ten business books for entrepreneurs. Rhonda also writes the nation's most widely circulated column on entrepreneurship and small business. Successful Business Strategies appears on USAToday.com and Inc.com and in more than one hundred newspapers, reaching millions of readers each week.

The Planning Shop's books have been adopted at more than four hundred business schools, colleges, and universities.

The Planning Shop's expanding line of business books includes:

- The **Successful Business series,** assisting entrepreneurs and business students in planning and growing businesses. Titles include *Six-Week Start-Up, What Business Should I Start?,* and *The Owner's Manual for Small Business.*

- The **In A Day series,** enabling entrepreneurs to tackle a critical business task and "Get it done right, get it done fast.™" Titles include *Business Plan In A Day, Winning Presentation In A Day,* and *Trade Show In A Day.*

- The **Better Business Bureau series,** helping entrepreneurs and consumers successfully make serious financial decisions. Titles include *Buying a Franchise, Buying a Home,* and *Starting an eBay Business.*

At The Planning Shop, now and in the future, you'll find a range of business resources. Learn more at *www.PlanningShop.com.*

Foreword
by Paul Orfalea,
Kinko's Founder & Author of *Copy This!*

In 1970, Paul Orfalea started his business with one copy machine in a tiny space carved out from a hamburger stand in Santa Barbara, California. From that, he built a copying empire, Kinko's, which was later acquired by FedEx for $2.4 billion.

Wouldn't it be nice if investors lined up to give you money, and the tough part of fundraising was deciding whose money to take? I've been on both sides of the business fundraising table, but building Kinko's was a little more luxurious than most experiences, because our co-workers were so eager to invest in the company. Rather than a franchise or corporate ownership structure, we created a series of partnerships. Each partnership owned the Kinko's stores in a geographic area.

Eventually, I had more than 200 partners in 127 partnerships. That's a lot of investor-partners, and there was no shortage of conflict. But there were also more eyes, ears, and ideas available. When you work with good partners, you're better able to stay focused on the big picture—to look ahead at ways to grow your company and deal with the major issues, not just the day-to-day problems. You're able to work "on" your business, not just "in" your business.

Fundraising is never easy. I know that from experience, because we had a very democratic structure at Kinko's, so I frequently had to sell 200 partners on the necessity of re-investing for growth. It takes more than persistence to raise the money you need. You need to know how to approach people, how to pitch yourself and your ideas, how to get to know the people you'll be asking for money and eventually working with.

After Kinko's, I started an investment firm called West Coast Asset Management. While the company focuses on public equities, we also receive many requests from private companies. My partners and I sort through numerous proposals every week, and I've been able to see what many entrepreneurs do right—and many more do wrong—when seeking money for their businesses.

As a prospective investor, I look for three things first:

1. I want a brief and clear presentation of what the business does, how it makes money, and how it makes money for investors.

2. Does the proposal ask for enough money? Liquidity is essential; those who try to impress me with frugality only seem unrealistic about the needs of a young business. I admire frugality, but I invest in reality.

3. Does the presenter look me in the eye, shake hands, and demonstrate conversational skills? I prefer to invest in people who function in the real world and are not completely myopic about their business. I want to see the right social skills for leadership.

Not all money is created equal; you want a good partner, not just a check. Think about how prospective investors treat you. Do they make you feel welcome by personally greeting you, offering refreshments, getting to know you? Or is your experience more like a cattle call? This reflects how you will be treated in the future. Don't just calculate how much money you need; define what kind of partner you can live with.

Finding an Angel Investor In A Day will help you realize your fundraising dreams. It will give you the tools you need, including methods you can use to find an angel, tips and tricks for making the best presentation you can, and even strategies to improve your negotiating skills.

Remember, partnerships start with little more than a handshake. And the best thing in life is making something out of nothing.

How to
Use This Book

To create *Finding an Angel Investor In A Day*, we gathered the most important and useful information about raising money from private investors from the people with real-life experience—angel investors, entrepreneurs who've raised money successfully, members of angel groups, and others who advise entrepreneurs on financing. We focused on what you need to know to locate and attract an angel investor and to understand the key terms you'll encounter in the process, especially in the early stages.

Finding an Angel Investor In A Day is organized in a step-by-step fashion, outlining the information you need to know during every stage of finding and securing an angel. While it is certainly useful (and recommended) to read this entire book regardless of how far along you are in the fundraising process, you may want to focus on different sections, depending on your particular situation:

- **If you're brand-new to the fundraising process**, you'll definitely want to follow this book from start to finish. Begin with Step 1 to learn what angels are looking for in an investment, whether an angel is right for you—and whether you are right for an angel.

- **If you don't know where to find a potential investor**, you'll be particularly interested in Step 2, which details how to locate an angel—whether an individual or an angel who is part of one of the increasingly popular angel groups.

- **If you've already identified an angel investor**, you may want to go straight to Step 3, which deals with how to prepare your company for the fundraising process, and Step 4, which gives guidance on how to successfully pitch your venture to an investor.

- **If you already have an angel who wants to invest in your company**, you might turn directly to Steps 5, 6, and 7, which deal with the all-important issues of valuation, negotiation, deal terms (including the term sheet), and the due diligence that angels will conduct on you and your business.

Once you are at the point of negotiating a deal with an angel, it's absolutely critical that you get a qualified securities attorney to help you with your own deal. While this book enables you to become comfortable with the key terms of investments, such deals are extremely complicated, with major financial and personal implications.

Using This Book

Throughout this book, you'll see worksheets and checklists you can use to write down the information to guide your own search to find and secure an investor. If there's not enough space on the worksheets, use a separate piece of paper to record your thoughts and data.

The Market

Use the following worksheet to prepare a market analysis. You'll use this data when you answer a potential angel's questions about the size, characteristics, and potential of your market.

Where is your target market located? (City? Country? Region? Urban? Suburban?)

What are the characteristics of your target customer? (Consumer customers: Age? Income range? Gender? Family size? Education? Business customers: Number of years in business? Number of employees? Industry?)

What motivates your customers to make purchases and what are their buying patterns?

What is the size of your market?

What have the growth rates been in your market for the last 5 years?

Evaluate Prospective Angel Groups

Fill out this worksheet to evaluate the groups you are considering or that you've approached. Make a copy for each group you evaluate.

Name of prospective angel investor group:

Proximity:

Investment dollar range:

Level of promised assistance:

Industry experience and contacts:

Relationship with lead angel or manager:

Investing history:

VC contacts:

Finding an Angel Investor
In A Day
Contents

1

STEP 1: What an Angel Investor Will Do for You

Accomplishments

In this Step you'll:

- ☐ 1. Discover how an angel investor can help your business succeed
- ☐ 2. Learn why angels invest
- ☐ 3. Find out what angels do
- ☐ 4. Learn how angel groups work
- ☐ 5. Discover the differences between angel investors and venture capitalists

Time-Saving Tools

You'll complete this Step more quickly if you have any of the following handy:

- ☐ 1. Your business plan
- ☐ 2. Your financial statements
- ☐ 3. An idea of how much money you need from an investor

Step 1:
What an Angel Investor Will Do for You

You have a great business idea. Perhaps you've invented a process that will revolutionize the dry cleaning industry, you've created a device that pet owners will find indispensable, or you've developed a software program that reduces home energy consumption. You've already written a business plan, researched the market, and assembled at least the beginning of a team. You may have designed a prototype or developed the product or service. You may even have reached the stage of attracting your first paying customers.

Your business is on the launch pad, ready for the countdown. All you need now is money to help your company take off and grow.

That's where an angel investor comes in. Angel investors are private individuals with money who are actively looking for opportunities to invest in promising young businesses like yours—companies founded on sound business ideas, which are likely to show significant, sustainable growth over the next three to seven years.

The best angel investors not only have money; they also have business and technical expertise, and contacts, and they will provide you with ongoing support. Find the right angel investor and you will not only receive the funds you need, you'll gain a valuable business partner.

QUICK**TIP**

Dumb Money vs. Smart Money

The investment community makes a distinction between "dumb" and "smart" money. Dumb money comes from someone who writes you a check but doesn't understand your industry or care to be involved in its strategic aspects. Smart money comes from people who take an active interest in the success of your business by providing support, including industry knowledge and contacts.

While an immediate infusion of cash can be tempting, starting a successful company takes tremendous effort and expertise. Go for the smart money. Being able to leverage an investor's expertise could mean the difference between success and failure.

1. What an angel brings to the table

Angel investors are just that: investors, not lenders. They provide interest-free money to entrepreneurs who are launching, expanding, or acquiring a business, in return for part of the ownership of that company.

Because angels are investors, not lenders, if a company fails, the entrepreneur does not need to repay the money. Since most new businesses are somewhat risky, not having to pay back the money if things don't work out is a very appealing concept for an entrepreneur. But angels know that new businesses are risky too, so before they invest, they'll want to know exactly how you plan to use their money in order to make your company grow. You'll need to show them a strong business plan, realistic financials, and a capable team. And after they invest, angels expect regular reports on the company's progress, as well as the chance to give their own input into how the business is run.

If a company succeeds, the angel investor gets a piece of its profits, a portion of the sale price of the company, and/or shares in the company if it should eventually go public on a stock exchange. As part owner of the company, the angel investor also acquires certain legal rights.

Typically, angels invest from $25,000 to $2,000,000 of their own money. But the best angel investors supply much more than cash. They also offer:

- **Business knowledge.** Angels often have many years' experience running and investing in companies. As the founder of a new company, you'll benefit from their business acumen. Use their expertise to fill in your knowledge base or the skill set of your management team.

- **Industry expertise.** In many cases, you're likely to find an angel in the same industry as your new business. They'll almost certainly have many years of experience, contacts, and a sound working understanding of how things really work in that industry.

- **Contacts.** Not only do angel investors provide advice, they also provide introductions. Their network will become your network. They can lead you to potential customers, suppliers, lenders, and key employees.

- **Support.** Angels are on your side. They want your business to succeed. And it's not just because they stand to gain financially from your success—angels take pleasure in seeing entrepreneurs and businesses flourish. Whether they are semi-retired, invest occasionally, or invest as a full-time profession, a good angel will make the time to support you and your business with technical knowledge, practical experience, and business advice.

- **Follow-on financing.** Angel investors can support your future fundraising efforts either by investing more of their own money or by helping you find additional angels or other sources of capital.

QUICK**TIP**

Bragging Rights

Some businesses are particularly "sexy" to investors. Angels who get involved in interesting companies—a restaurant, a winery, a minor-league sports team—will have a built-in conversation topic at cocktail parties and dinners with friends and business associates. They'll also have their eye on the perks—the best table in "their" restaurant, the owners' box at the game, or their name on the label of a good Pinot Noir!

2. Why angels invest

The primary reason angel investors invest in entrepreneurial businesses is to make money. They will evaluate any business proposal first and foremost on financial criteria. Generally, they must feel confident that they will see a higher rate of return on their money by investing in your company than by investing in less risky alternatives, such as stocks and bonds. But other factors motivate angel investors as well, including:

- **The thrill of entrepreneurship.** Many angels are former entrepreneurs, and they enjoy participating in the launch of a successful company, the competitive nature of business, and the challenge of the marketplace.

- **A desire to support their community.** Angels want to contribute to the growth of the local economy. They recognize that new businesses—their investments—have a positive impact on the community by creating new jobs and revitalizing industries.

- **The search for a balanced investment portfolio.** Angels are high-net-worth individuals and generally have other investments, such as real estate, stocks, and bonds. They may be motivated to invest in high-growth, high-risk new companies to diversify their portfolios.

- **The need to be engaged.** For angels who are retired or semi-retired, investing in young businesses is a method of staying involved in the business community in an interesting way that suits their lifestyle.

- **A wish to keep learning.** Angel investors tend to be intellectually curious. Being involved with new companies enables them to continue to learn and acquire knowledge about business and industry.

3. What's an angel investor?

QUICK**TIP**

What's in a Name?

The term *angel investor* originated in the early twentieth century and referred to people who invested in Broadway shows, seeking a little glamour in their lives, along with a return on their investment—think *The Producers*, but the scrupulous version.

Angel investors are individuals or groups of individuals who invest *their own money* in a new business. It is important to distinguish them from other types of investors, such as venture capitalists (see pages 15-18), who invest other people's money.

Angels provide funds for promising businesses, generally in the early stages of development. They typically invest at least $25,000, and sometimes much more, in fledging enterprises. Of course, others may also invest in your business—a rich friend or relative, for instance, may invest $5,000 or $10,000 to help you pursue your dream. But generally, these are not considered to be angel investors because their primary motive may not be a return on their financial investment.

Angel investors expect to realize a significant—and relatively rapid—return on their investment. In return for their money, angels take partial ownership, or *equity*, of your company. Money from angels is *not* a loan. It does not need to be repaid if the business fails. Instead, angels will make their money back, ideally with substantial profits, when you sell the business, go public, merge with another company, or provide another way for them to take their money out (that is, a *liquidity event*). In some cases, angels may receive a piece of ongoing operating profits.

Because angels expect a dramatic return in a relatively short period of time, they look for:

- Businesses in high-growth markets

- A true competitive edge

- A proven management team

- A clear exit strategy—a plan for how the entrepreneur, management team, employees, and investors will realize their profit

- Companies whose value will be increased by the addition of their money

- Evidence of founder's investment in, and commitment to, the company

The Right Time to Seek an Angel Investor Is When:

- You are willing to give up some ownership of your company.

- You have a compelling business plan.

- You have a business concept with very high growth potential—enough not only to sustain the business but also to produce substantial profits for investors.

- You have a product or service that is developed or near completion.

- You have exhausted other funding sources, such as personal savings, credit cards, a mortgage on your home, and funds from friends and family.

- You don't want to incur further debt (by re-mortgaging your house, for instance).

QUICK**TIP**

Money from Family and Friends

If your wealthy father-in-law or best friend wants to invest in your start-up, it's tempting to accept this readily available capital. But think carefully before you accept money from friends or family, especially if you also have the potential to raise money from outside angel investors. Not only may holiday dinners become very awkward if they lose their money, but having many small investors early in your company's development can complicate later deals if you seek outside investors.

What Do Angels Invest In?

Angels invest in a broad array of businesses, from technology to medical equipment to software companies to business-to-business firms to online retail to restaurants to enterprises selling new inventions. In fact, angels invest in virtually every kind of business—as long as there's a potential for significant financial returns. So whether you are the president of a technology start-up in New Jersey or an entrepreneur in Idaho with a smart idea for a new piece of farming equipment, there's likely to be an angel investor in your backyard.

Angel investors are interested in businesses that have the potential for substantial growth and are likely to produce hefty profit margins or to be an acquisition target within a few years. Because of this, industries with high growth potential have attracted the most angel investment. The chart on page 10 shows which industry sectors attracted the most angel investment in the U.S. in 2005.

Since many angels made their money in high technology, and technology-based businesses have shown fast growth and rapid returns, a large percentage of angels are attracted to businesses that include a technological component in their concept or operation.

This isn't to say that other types of businesses won't catch an angel's attention. It's all in the business model. An attractive business is one that has a good chance of providing high financial returns for an investor, not just for the business owner. A corner coffee shop many provide a good income for its owner/operator, but for an angel to be interested in investing, it has to have a more ambitious business plan—perhaps one that includes creating a franchise operation. Stand-alone small businesses, even if their chances of success are good, typically do not generate the kind of financial returns that make them attractive to angel investors.

Share of Angel Investment in the U.S. by Sector, 2005

SECTOR	PERCENTAGE OF OVERALL ANGEL INVESTMENT
Healthcare services/medical devices and equipment	20%
Software	18%
Biotechnology	12%
Electronics/Hardware	8%
Media	6%
Industrial/Energy	6%
IT	6%

Source: Jeffrey E. Sohl, University of New Hampshire, Center for Venture Research

4. What's an angel group?

When angels join forces and combine their investment dollars, they are known as an angel group (or *network*). These groups review new business opportunities and invest collectively as a unit or, more typically, as individuals. In 2005 there were more than 250 well-established angel groups across the United States, with an average membership of forty-one individual investors.

The majority of angel groups hold regular meetings, often monthly lunches. Most bring together investors to hear entrepreneurs present their business ideas. Members of the group then discuss the merits of the business concept, giving feedback and suggestions. Then individual investors decide whether or not they want to invest their own money in the venture.

Most angel groups have established application procedures —some are stricter and more formal than others. Some groups have websites spelling out their application and pre- sentation processes. Others require a member of the group to sponsor you if you want to apply or make a presentation.

Individual members of the group may have responsibility for screening entrepreneurs and business plans before they are presented to the entire group. The Rockies Venture Club, based in Denver, Colorado, does screening in this way. In the case of other groups, a professional manager is hired to screen applications from entrepreneurs. And then there are groups like the Boston-based Common Angels, which has a professionally managed fund and a full-time, dedicated staff.

QUICK**TIP**

Your Angel Is Close By

It used to be that angels would only invest in businesses that were no more than half a day's drive from their home. Angels like to be close to their investments; they want to be involved in business decisions and stay abreast of company developments. Today, sophis- ticated angels will take a short plane ride for the right invest- ment opportunity, but most investments are still made locally.

A few groups work more like venture capital firms by pooling members' funds or even raising money, which they then use to invest collectively in business opportunities, rather than having each member of the group decide whether they want to invest individually (a much more common approach).

Angel networks like to receive business plans and applications, especially from promising companies. They believe that the more investment opportunities they see, the more potential there is to find high-quality deals (this is referred to as *quality deal flow)*. The New York Angels, for example, receives thousands of applications for funds each year. Of those, approximately three companies are invited to present to the group's members every month.

Working with an angel investor group, rather than an individual investor, presents both advantages and disadvantages. An angel group has more capital to invest, so if you need to raise a lot of money (more than $100,000 or so), you may be better off approaching a group instead of an individual investor.

Angel groups have more collective investment experience, and they are concerned about their reputation in the entrepreneurial community (to ensure quality deal flow). So they are likely to offer you a fair, if not always the most competitive, deal. On the other hand, an angel group may use its clout to negotiate terms that are tougher for you than a solo angel would.

You may also find it more difficult to form a strong personal connection with a member of a group assigned to your company than you would with an individual angel who you know relates to the challenges you are facing.

Finally, some angel groups may act more like venture capital firms and make more stringent demands of you than individual angel investors normally do, such as asking you to agree that you can be replaced as CEO. Understanding the differences between angel groups and solo angels will help you find the right match for your company.

Angel Groups at Work:
A Snapshot

- Angel groups meet regularly (often once a month) to review business proposals from entrepreneurs.

- The average investment for an angel group is $100,000 to $2 million, compared to $25,000 to $100,000 for an individual angel.

- In the majority of cases, individual angels in the group make their own decisions about whether to invest in a particular company. However, some angel groups create a fund in which individual angels pool their money, and they then take a majority vote on whether to invest in a deal.

- Many angel groups invest in a broad range of industries and assign the management of particular investments—in retail, manufacturing, or telecommunications businesses—to group members with relevant industry experience.

- Some groups have particular specialties. BioAngels in Chicago invests in medical and life sciences businesses in the Midwest, for example.

- The number of applications an angel group receives depends on its size and location. A large group, like Common Angels in Boston, considers several dozen business plans every month, while a smaller one in a less populated city might see fewer than ten applications a month from entrepreneurs.

5. Understand the differences between angel investors and venture capitalists

Although they both invest in entrepreneurial companies, angel investors and venture capitalists (VCs) are not the same. Understanding the differences between them will help you decide which you should seek for your business. The key differences between the two types of investors include:

- **Whose money they invest.** Angels invest their own money. VCs invest other people's money. This is a critical distinction and colors all the decisions angel investors and VCs make.

  VCs raise money for funds ($100 million or more is not unusual for a single fund) from large institutional investors, pension funds, and extremely wealthy individuals. (Capital provided by venture capitalists is sometimes referred to as "institutional" capital.) They must show *very* high financial returns to these investors. Angels, on the other hand, are not under pressure to make money for other people. They can trust their own instincts and take more risks.

- **How much they invest.** Typically, individual angels invest from $25,000 to $100,000, while angel groups invest $100,000 to $2 million. VCs, on the other hand, routinely invest more than a few million dollars, even in early-stage companies. Since they know some of these companies will go bust, VCs need the other companies in their portfolios to be huge hits to balance their returns.

- **Size of the potential businesses.** Both VCs and angels seek businesses with high growth potential, but because of their responsibilities to their own investors, VCs need to find companies with the possibility of extraordinarily high growth, a minimum of $50 million to $100 million within a few years.

- **When they invest.** While both angels and VCs will invest in companies at any stage of development, angels are more likely to invest in younger companies. "Seed" funding—given in the very earliest stages, when a company is still developing a prototype, refining a business concept, and researching a market—is more likely to be appropriate for angels than for VCs. VCs are increasingly investing in later-stage companies, to reduce their risk.

- **Decision-making process.** VCs almost always make group decisions, with all members of the VC firm weighing in on an investment. Angel investors can make individual decisions.

- **Relationship to founder.** VCs typically see their role as bringing in professional management to the companies they invest in. They're far more likely to replace the founders of a company with experienced CEOs and managers. Angels, by contrast, expect founders to stay in key management positions, if not to run the company.

Key Differences between Angel Investors and Venture Capitalists

	ANGEL INVESTOR	VENTURE CAPITALIST
Investment criteria	Growth company	Extremely high-growth company
Source of investment dollars	Personal assets	Other people's money; institutional funds
Investment range	$25,000–$2,000,000	$5,000,000+
Expected return	3–10 times original investment	5–10 times original investment
Typical stage of investment	Seed, start-up, or early	High-growth start-up and expansion
What they bring to the deal	Early funding and hands-on expertise	Large amounts of money, team building, industry-specific strengths
Extent of due diligence (See pages 131-136 for more on due diligence)	Some to significant	Significant to huge amount
Will they replace founder as CEO?	Less likely	More likely
Number of deals	1–3 per year	15–18 per fund per year

The Funding Gap

As the chart above reveals, there is a gap between the largest average sum an individual angel will offer and the smallest average amount a venture capitalist firm will invest. The gap begins at $500,000 or less and goes as high as $5 million. This funding gap is often filled by angel groups, who are able to invest higher sums than individual angels but less money than the average venture capitalist. Companies that fall into the funding gap may have a harder time raising money than companies on either side.

Investment Timeline

When in the life of your business is it the right time to approach an angel investor—and when is it better to approach a venture capitalist? This chart shows the typical business stages that angels and VCs invest in.

STAGE OF COMPANY DEVELOPMENT	COMPANY ACTIVITY	TIMEFRAME	BEST INVESTOR
Seed	Idea/market/ product research	< 1 year	Angel investor
Start-up	Beta product	< 18 months	Angel investor
High-growth start-up	Proof of concept	< 18 months	Venture capitalist
Early stage	First sale/contract	1–3 years	Angel/Venture capitalist
Expansion stage	Rapid growth	< 3 years	Venture capitalist/ Angel group
Later stage	Global expansion, acquiring other companies	> 3 years	Venture capitalist
Exit	Positioning for company sale or IPO	>3 years	Venture capitalist

2

Accomplishments

In this Step you'll:

☐ 1. Learn how to use networking to locate potential angels

☐ 2. Discover where else to look for angels

☐ 3. Learn how to evaluate prospective individual angels

☐ 4. Discover where to find angel groups

☐ 5. Learn how to evaluate prospective angel groups

Time-Saving Tools

You'll complete this Step more quickly if you have any of the following handy:

☐ 1. List of your business, industry, professional, and social contacts

☐ 2. List of associations in your industry

☐ 3. List of trade journals, to look for conferences and contacts

Step 2:
How to Find an Angel Investor

Ten years ago, tracking down an angel investor was difficult if you didn't live in the Silicon Valley or Boston's Route 128 corridor. Even in those locations, it was a case of "who you knew" through business or social connections that led to finding an angel. Today, the angel investor universe is more mature and structured. There are active angels across the U.S. in communities of all sizes, from Chippewa Valley to Chicago. If you have a good concept—and a willingness to do a little research—you can find an angel.

But finding the *right* angel is as important as finding *an* angel. It helps to know what to look for when angel hunting. As you begin your search, the first thing to look for is an angel with sufficient funds to invest in a relatively high-risk venture (as any new business is). But money isn't everything. Most angels invest only in local companies, and you'll need to have a number of face-to-face meetings both while trying to secure funding and once you have an investor. So look for angels who are geographically nearby. Next, seek angels who come from the industry in which your business is operating. Angels who have worked in your industry are valuable because they offer first-hand experience and expertise that you can use. Since they are already well networked, they can provide introductions to potential customers, partners, vendors, and suppliers. They're also more likely to understand your business concept and its potential.

QUICK**TIP**

More Is Better

The expression "Don't put all your eggs in one basket" holds particularly true when you start looking for an angel investor. Having multiple parties interested in your business makes it more attractive to investors and gives you leverage when negotiating the terms of the deal. Cast your net wide and look for a number of individual angels and angel groups simultaneously.

Who Can Invest in My Company?

Before approaching an angel, you'll need to determine whether they have enough money to invest in your company—and, just as important—whether they can afford to lose it. Imagine if you were depending on an infusion of cash to start manufacturing your first product or to launch your website and your angel couldn't come up with the promised funds. All your hard work, and your company, could go down the drain.

One way to reassure yourself about a potential investor's financial condition is to determine whether they meet established accreditation criteria. This means they fit certain categories outlined by the U.S. Securities and Exchange Commission (SEC). The SEC defines an accredited investor as one whose individual net worth, or joint net worth with a spouse, is in excess of $1 million, or one whose income has exceeded $200,000 in the past two years or whose joint income with a spouse was more than $300,000 in the past two years—and who has a reasonable expectation of reaching the same income level in the current year.

In some cases, especially if you are raising many millions of dollars, many of your investors will have to meet the SEC's criteria of being "accredited investors." Only your attorney, one who is experienced in securities law, can advise you on this. For more information on SEC accreditation, including who is exempt from the definition, visit *www.sec.gov/answers/accred.htm.*

While the SEC's definition of "accredited investor" is still in use, it dates back many years and experts argue that a more realistic evaluation of a person who can afford to lose money by investing in new ventures would put the net worth of the average angel in the $3 million–to–$5 million range.

Your angel investor may not fit the SEC criteria but may still be a good bet. Your rich Uncle Bob, for example, may not be worth $1 million, but he might have extra money; be willing to risk it on you, his favorite relative; and believe in you and your business idea.

It's not always easy to find out about an angel investor's financial status. Do what you can to reassure yourself. See page 38 for more on how to conduct "due diligence" on potential investors.

1. Networking

Networking to find an angel works best when you approach it in an organized fashion. Evaluate everyone you know as a potential investor—or, more likely, as a *connection* to a potential investor. Make a list of the people you know who can either help you directly or lead you to someone who can.

Go through your address book, database, and contact management program. Begin with any current or professional connections, past employers, employees, and colleagues. Go through lists from any organizations you belong to: alumni associations; churches, synagogues, or mosques; community or entrepreneurial organizations; even your children's school associations.

Keep all potential doors open when thinking about people who might lead you to an angel investor. They are not always the obvious choices, such as bankers and lawyers. Your child's soccer coach, your golfing buddy, or even a book club member may know just the right investor for you.

Go to conferences and events where potential investors or industry experts will attend or speak on panels. Talk to them at coffee breaks or over lunch and tell them about your business. Even if they aren't the right match for you, they may know of an investor who is. Identify potential investors the same way you would potential customers—cast your net wide!

Think about groups in your community with which you would have a natural affinity, because of shared interests, beliefs, or background: businesswomen's organizations, a local Hispanic entrepreneurship group, or a gay business persons' forum. Groups like these may also have leads for you.

How Long Will It Take?

Finding an angel investor takes time. The time you spend looking for investment funds is time spent away from running your business. Factor this into your planning and consider delegating some, or possibly all, of the fundraising work to one of your partners or a trusted advisor.

Find angels and set up meetings	Meet with angels	Negotiate terms	Due diligence/ Draft final documents	Total time
1–4 months	3–6 months	1–3 months	1–3 months	6–16 months

Begin with People You Know

Start close to home when you begin networking and approach:

- Your accountant

- Your financial planner or financial planners you know

- Your attorney or an attorney you know who specializes in investments

- Your banker

- Any high-net-worth individuals you know

- Business owners

- People you know who have already secured angel investment or venture capital

Remember, these people may or may not be potential angel investors themselves. However, they may lead you to others they know who *are* potential angel investors.

The Approach

Call or email your contacts and tell them you'd like to take them to lunch and ask their advice and get their input about a business you're in the process of developing. If you are speaking with them on the phone, they may want to know right away what you have in mind, so have a succinct description of your business concept prepared to pique their interest. Your goal, however, is to meet with them in person. They're more likely to spend the time thinking of people who might help you when you're in their presence.

Don't be surprised if they ask you to send your business plan or an executive summary to determine whether they're interested in talking further with you or helping you network to find angels (see pages 54-55 for more on preparing a business plan and executive summary).

Once you've secured the appointment, take a printed version of your business plan to leave with your potential angel. It's also a good idea to take a PowerPoint presentation that gives an overview of your business concept and market. (See pages 61-90 for more on presenting your business concept.)

What to Ask

When you're meeting with people who can lead you to potential angel investors—or who are potential investors themselves—ask them some or all of the following:

- I'm looking for an investor in my business. Do you know anyone who might be interested?

- Have you ever been an angel investor or invested in someone else's business?

- Would you consider looking at my business plan?

- Did someone invest in your business to help you get started? Do you think that person might be interested in investing in my business?

- Are any of your clients/customers active in investing in new companies? Would you be willing to introduce me to them or to send them my business plan?

- Do you know of anyone else I should speak to? May I use your name when I contact them?

- Would you consider passing my business plan on to some people who might be interested in investing in my business?

- What might it take to have you invest in my business?

- Do you have any advice for me?

Be sure to follow up! Send thank you notes to everyone you've spoken with, even if they did not have any names for you at that point. You never know who they'll think of later. And get in touch with any contacts they suggest.

Get an Introduction

By far the best way to approach an individual angel or an angel group is through a personal introduction. Being referred by someone known to the angel investor provides you with a degree of credibility. And angels are more likely to invest if you come recommended by people they know and trust. Some, including certain angel groups, will consider your proposal only if it comes via a personal recommendation or a member of the angel group.

However, having another person approach an investor on your behalf means that someone else is presenting your business idea. As helpful as your referral source will be, they won't necessarily understand your business as well as you do and may unwittingly misrepresent you.

To help them represent you properly, give them a written copy of your "elevator pitch"—that is, a brief description of your business that could be given in the time it takes to ride up a few floors in an elevator. The elevator pitch describes your company's product or service, your market, and your competitive advantages. Encourage your contact to use this pitch whenever they approach a potential investor.

Your referee's initial conversation with a potential investor might start something like this:

"Helen, I want to ask you to look at a new business opportunity. I know the founder, and I think the business may be of interest to you. It's a new franchise concept in the travel industry, focused on adventure tourism for the huge baby boomer market, which is just reaching retirement and traveling in record numbers. One of the founders started another company, which was later acquired, and the other was a key executive at a travel company. I'd like you to meet them. Can they give you a call?"

QUICK**TIP**

The Best Person for the Job

The founder of a company is almost always the best person to go out and network with potential investors. But if you truly aren't confident enough in your communication skills to find, and then negotiate with, an angel investor, choose someone on your team or a trusted advisor who does have these capabilities to act in this capacity for your business.

2. Where else to look for individual angel investors

Don't limit your quest for potential investors to just the people you know. Broaden your search by looking for potential angel investors in:

- **Investment forums.** Investment forums are held to bring investors together with entrepreneurs looking for funding. These forums might be organized by entrepreneur associations, business organizations, entrepreneurship departments at universities, the media, or chambers of commerce. They generally include presentations by pre-selected entrepreneurs, talks by investors, and/or training sessions in fundraising presentations.

- **Entrepreneurs' organizations.** Many communities, especially larger cities, have organizations composed of entrepreneurs. They hold regular meetings to exchange information, ideas, and contacts. Find out if there are any in your area by looking for nearby entrepreneur groups on the Internet or in the press or by inquiring at your local Small Business Development Center or Chamber of Commerce (see page 29).

- **Trade and professional associations.** No matter what your industry, there's almost certainly an association composed of other businesses in that field. Frequently, these associations have local chapters that hold regular meetings, where you can network with other entrepreneurs to help identify investors active in your industry. You can find a list of many industry associations on The Planning Shop's website at *www.PlanningShop.com/associations*.

QUICK**TIP**

Ask Angels for Advice

If you've contacted a potential angel investor and they've passed on the opportunity to invest in your business either because they're committed to other companies or don't feel they know your industry well enough, you can still ask them to serve as an informal advisor. Their business knowledge could be invaluable—and you may be able to return to them later for follow-on investments.

- **Small Business Development Centers (SBDCs).** SBDCs provide free one-on-one counseling and low-cost training programs to entrepreneurs. Find one near you at *www.asbdc-us.org.* Make an appointment with an SBDC counselor and tell them about your business plans. They'll educate you about the different kinds of funding available to entrepreneurs.

- **Chambers of Commerce.** Contact your local Chamber of Commerce to find out about events they have planned for businesspeople in your community, where you can network for potential investors.

- **Trade shows and relevant conferences.** Learn about conferences in your industry by going to the websites of your trade association, reading trade publications, and getting on the email event lists of local business schools and the SBDC. Attend as many events as you can and network with other attendees and speakers at breaks between sessions.

- **Trade press for your industry.** Read relevant industry magazines or newspapers to keep up-to-date with news and trends. These publications provide leads for potential angel investors. Make note of who is being quoted and where they work. Add them to your list of people to contact.

- **Incubators.** Business incubators offer support to start-up companies by providing entrepreneurs with resources and services. Services include management guidance, technical assistance, rental space, shared business services and equipment, and assistance in obtaining financing. Visit the National Business Incubation Association at *http://www. nbia.org/index.php* to find local incubators. Research their offerings to determine whether their services are what you need.

- **Business schools.** Many business schools offer programs and events for entrepreneurs. Contact schools in your area and find out what classes, lectures, and other events you can attend (some are for students only). Business professors are well connected to local companies and business leaders, and if your business looks promising to them, they may be able to provide introductions to potential investors.

How Many Angels Do You Need?

The number of angels your business needs depends on a number of factors:

- Does your angel have adequate funds to finance you until the next stage of your business development? If an angel is able to offer you only part of the sum of money you need, approach other investors to make up the difference and ask your existing angel to help you approach other investors.

- Does your angel have enough funds for additional rounds of financing? If you have more than one investor, you will have more opportunities if you need additional funds down the line.

- Does your angel have contacts within the angel and venture-capital community to find follow-on investors? If not, you may want to bring other angels on board who do. This way, you'll improve your chances of securing money, should you need it, at later stages of your company's development.

3. Evaluate your prospective individual angel investors

If you are fortunate enough to have identified a number of potential angel investors, it's important to evaluate the ones you consider to be your best prospects. Use the worksheet on page 33 to record data about the angel investors you have contacted or researched. The more positive data you record, the better the possibility that the angel is a good match for you. Consider the following when completing the worksheet:

- **Proximity.** Most angels invest only in local businesses. They want to be close enough to drop by for meetings and progress reports and to check out the operations.

- **Net worth.** Does this angel have enough money to fund you comfortably? Are they likely to have the money for future rounds of investment?

- **Know/trust.** Do you have a prior history with the investor? Did you work together before? Were they helpful and communicative? Mutual trust is a very big advantage.

- **Comfortable with risk.** Try to ascertain whether this investor is nervous about investing their money—money they could lose. This is particularly important if you are approaching a first-time investor. You don't want a fretful angel breathing down your neck.

- **Industry experience and contacts.** Has this investor worked in your industry? If so, they will have a better understanding of the issues you may face, and they are likely to have contacts that can open doors for you.

- **Investing history.** Have they invested in companies before? Are any similar to yours? What is their track record?

- **Background.** What types of positions has this investor held in the past? Does their background help your business? Can they provide advice or part-time assistance in areas where you may be weak, such as finance or marketing?

- **VC contacts.** If an angel knows venture capitalists, they may be able to assist you with follow-on rounds of funding if your company has large growth potential.

- **References.** Speak to other companies this angel has invested in and to business professionals they have worked with. Try to find out how hands-on they are with the companies they invest in. How much attention—or interference—will they give you?

Compatibility Tests

You may find an angel or angel group that meets all your requirements on paper and is ready to invest in your business. But before you take the plunge, make sure that they are a good fit with you personally.

You're going to be working closely with your angel for a long time. It's almost certain that you'll have to make some tough business and financial decisions together. When things get rough—and there are rough times in virtually every business—you'll have to deal with your investors. Make sure your angel is someone you feel you can talk with, someone who shares your vision, and someone who has the patience and personality to work through challenges with you as a partner.

Availability of funds and experience in your industry are great assets, but if you don't "click" with an angel right away, spend more time together to get to know them better before you make a long-term commitment.

Evaluate Prospective Individual Angel Investors

Fill out this worksheet help you to evaluate the investors you are considering or that you've approached. Make a copy for each angel you evaluate.

Name of prospective angel investor:

Proximity:

Net worth:

Know/trust:

Comfort with risk:

Industry experience and contacts:

Investing history:

Background:

VC contacts:

References:

QUICK**TIP**

The Kauffman Foundation

The Ewing Marion Kauffman Foundation (*www.kauffman. org*) works on the advancement of entrepreneurship by, among other things, offering education and training programs and promoting entrepreneurship-friendly policies. The Foundation's website includes reports and latest news on many entrepreneurship-related topics. It's a very useful resource for entrepreneurs.

4. How to find an angel group

The best place to find an angel group is on the Internet. Almost all angel groups have websites that provide information on how they operate, who their members are, their investment criteria, and how you can apply to them for funds.

The following organizations are essential resources when you are looking for an angel group. They provide online directories of angel groups, including links to their websites, and they are excellent sources of information on how angel groups operate:

- **Angel Capital Association (ACA)** *www.angelcapitalassociation. org*. This is North America's professional association of angel groups. Its 200 members in the U.S. and Canada share best practices and develop data about the angel investing field.

  While it principally serves its membership of angel investors, the ACA is a valuable resource for entrepreneurs because it maintains a directory of angel groups, as well as a listing of national organizations that have directories of investors who provide matching services for entrepreneurs and angels.

- The **Angel Capital Education Foundation (ACEF)** *www.angelcapitaleducation.org*. This is a non-profit organization devoted to the education of angel investors. It collects and disseminates data and information on angel investors and angel groups. The programs of the ACEF include educational workshops and seminars. Its website includes a directory of angel groups and a dedicated resources section for entrepreneurs.

Are Finders Keepers?

Finders, or financial matchmakers, are intermediaries (usually business professionals such as accountants, insurance brokers, and retired executives) who connect entrepreneurs with investors for a fee. They focus on the $100,000 to $2 million investment range. If you are considering hiring a finder, keep in mind:

- An angel investor will view finders negatively. Some may feel this is a job you should have been able to do yourself. No angel wants a portion of the money they are investing to go to paying a finder. They want *all* their funds to be invested in your business.

- Under U.S. Securities and Exchange Commission (SEC) regulations, most finders should be registered as securities brokers/dealers. However, many are not and their skills and quality vary widely. To find a legitimate matchmaker, ask business acquaintances for recommendations. Once you have found a potential matchmaker, ask for multiple references and follow up carefully.

- Most finders charge a fee of up to 10% of the funds raised. Retainers, upfront fees, and equity participation are also options. Be wary of large front-end fees or commissions exceeding 10%.

QUICK**TIP**

Be Careful

Be cautious about using any finder! There are many frauds who prey on entrepreneurs. They'll gladly take your money and promise they'll find you the angel investor of your dreams. They won't. Bear in mind that in some cases payments to a finder can violate securities laws. An early-stage funding deal that is illegal will come back to haunt you later. At the very least, check with a securities lawyer before signing any finder's or matchmaker's contract.

5. Evaluate prospective angel groups

It's important to evaluate the angel groups you consider to be your best prospects. Use the worksheet on page 37 to record data about the groups you have contacted or researched. The more positive data you record, the better the possibility that the group is a good match for you. Consider the following when completing the worksheet:

- **Proximity.** Like individual angel investors, most angel groups invest only in local businesses.

- **Investment dollar range.** Do you fit their investment parameters? Most groups have minimum and maximum investment sums.

- **Level of promised assistance.** Does the group provide nothing but money or do they offer hands-on assistance? How much?

- **Industry experience and contacts.** Do the members of this group have experience within your industry? Do they understand the issues you'll be facing? Will they be able to open doors for you?

- **Investing history.** What has this group invested in before? How many companies? Are there any similar to yours? How experienced is the network with investing?

- **Relationship with lead angel or manager.** How well do you get along with this group's key contact person? Do you respect them? Can you learn from them? Do they appear to respect you and deal with you professionally?

- **VC contacts.** You may want follow-on funding from a venture capitalist at a later stage in your company's growth. Does the angel group have established relationships with any VCs?

- **Other companies they have invested in.** Do the other companies this group has invested in have value to you? Will they be able to provide a business model, guidance, or business opportunities?

- **References.** To collect references, speak to the founders of other companies this group has invested in, VCs they have worked with, and attorneys or accountants who know them.

Evaluate Prospective Angel Groups

Fill out this worksheet to help you evaluate the groups you are considering or that you've approached. Make a copy for each group you evaluate.

Name of prospective angel investor group:

Proximity:

Investment dollar range:

Level of promised assistance:

Industry experience and contacts:

Relationship with lead angel or manager:

Investing history:

VC contacts:

Other companies they have invested in:

References:

Due Diligence

Just as an angel investor will conduct due diligence on you and your business before deciding to invest (see pages 131-136), you should carry out a measure of due diligence on any prospective angel investor. The most important fact you need to confirm is whether they actually have the funds to support your venture.

You can do background research—on the Internet, at the library, using the resources of industry and trade associations, and by talking to your potential angel's business and personal contacts, including any other entrepreneurs they have invested with. It's also important to ask some direct questions. Often, it's less uncomfortable to have a professional associated with you—your business lawyer, accountant, or securities attorney—ask some of the due diligence questions of your investor. Having them make these inquiries can prevent you from endangering your relationship with your investor.

You—or your advisors—may ask your angel for:

- References (personal, professional, other angels, prior angel investments)

- Previous companies owned

- Previous employers

- Previous or pending lawsuits

- A list of all previous angel activity, the status of that activity, and contact information for the principals involved

Accomplishments

In this Step you'll:

☐ 1. Discover what types of businesses attract angel investors

☐ 2. Discover what types of markets appeal to angels

☐ 3. Find out what angels want to know about you

☐ 4. Find out what angels want to know about your team

☐ 5. Discover the secrets of a killer business plan

☐ 6. Understand exit strategies and why they matter to angels

Time-Saving Tools

You'll complete this Step more quickly if you have any of the following handy:

☐ Data about your business concept, market, and competition

☐ Résumés for you and your team members

☐ An up-to-date business plan

☐ Your financial statements

Step 3:
Make Yourself a Good Catch

Once you've found an angel, what will make them actually invest in your company? How will you make them notice you and how will you then convince them that yours is a company they want to invest in? Remember that many angels, especially sophisticated ones, see a lot of deals. And every entrepreneur who presents an investment opportunity believes theirs is a "can't miss" idea.

Even those angels who don't receive many proposals for new ventures have many other, much safer, options for investing their money. So an investor doesn't need a specific reason to turn you down or even to skip meeting with you or reading your business plan. That's why you have to make yourself, your business opportunity, and your business plan, compelling.

The best way to do that is to be prepared. The more complete the package that you present, the more you'll stand out from the crowd of money-seekers. Moreover, the stronger your presentation and the better prepared you are, the more an angel investor will be confident in your ability to build a company.

So pull it all together—the concept, the leadership, the business plan, the financials, and all the supporting documents you'll need—and prepare to show your angel why your business is the smartest investment they can make.

QUICK**TIP**

More Than Just a Pretty Face

Courting an angel is somewhat like dating. An angel may be attracted to you based on first impressions—your business idea looks intriguing or your background is impressive. But for them to keep calling, you need the whole package: concept, team, market, financials, and business plan.

1. The right business idea

You know you have a great business concept, but is it the right kind of business for an angel investor? Whether your business is still in the planning stages or you're already in production, you have to prove to an angel investor that it has the potential to become *very* successful and sustainable. Your investor must see your business as a compelling opportunity.

What makes a business idea appealing to an angel investor?

- **Compelling, executable business idea.** The basis for the business itself must be solid. You must have a truly effective and impressive product or service that fills a real need in the market. And you must be able to build a business around it in a reasonable period of time with a reasonable amount of money.

- **Large market and rapid, high-growth potential.** There are business concepts that might provide a good income for you but won't provide enough revenue and profits for an investor. An investor will be looking for a speedy, high return on the funds they put into your business.

- **Growing industry.** Your business needs to be in an industry that is growing rapidly, rather than one that has matured or is in decline. Your proposal will be even more attractive if you are in an industry your potential angel investor understands and/or is excited about.

- **It's a business, not just a product.** A song is a product; a music publishing company is a business. Sometimes a good product idea is not sufficient to support an entire business. Many improvements to existing products sell well but are not enough to sustain a company in the long term. Angels are looking for whole businesses.

- **In the right stage of development.** If you are looking for seed or start-up money to launch your business or create a prototype or if you need funds for marketing or key staffing for expansion, you are in the right development stage for angel investment.

The Value
of Your Ideas

Depending on what type of business you are running, you may have *intellectual property* (IP) that you'll need to consider protecting. Intellectual property is composed of those intangible aspects of a company that make it truly unique and give it a competitive edge. These could be ideas, data, designs, or processes—anything that is the product of the mind, rather than physical property.

Intellectual property could be a secret ingredient for your new skincare cream or the computer code for your software. It might also be the name of your product, a logo (Nike's "swoosh"), or a slogan (like UPS's "What can Brown do for you?")

Intellectual property is viewed as a company asset, often a very valuable one, and can be protected by law. The most common forms of protection are trademarks, copyrights, and patents. Securing these, especially patents, costs money, often a lot of money. Defending your rights against other companies' encroachment on your intellectual property can be particularly expensive. It's conceivable that your seed funding round may be concentrated on raising money to protect your IP.

Angel investors will want to know if you have patents, copyrights, or trademarks. Many angels prefer to invest in companies with substantial intellectual property. Some will favor protecting that property, while others will believe that patenting an idea or product will only draw your competitors' attention to your product. There are also those who feel that a patent is only as valuable as the amount of money you have set aside to defend it.

- **Money will be used for growth.** You are seeking financing to develop, grow, and expand a business, not money to get an existing business out of debt. Angel investors are not a good source of money for turning around failing companies.

- **Capable entrepreneur and strong team.** You have assembled a quality team of professionals, including yourself, capable of both developing the product and managing the company. Angel investors, much more than venture capitalists, expect the founders of the company to be able to lead the company for at least the first years of development.

- **Original, but not completely new, idea.** Why not a truly new and groundbreaking concept? Because a novel product or invention requires too large a budget to build a market—to educate customers on how the concept works and why they need it. Sometimes it pays *not* to be first. Let the first or second company into the market pay the costs associated with launching a new product, and *then* bring in an improved version.

- **Clear concept communicated succinctly.** You'll need to convey your idea simply and concisely, even if you have a complex product or concept. An angel will not invest in your business if they don't understand it or if they see it has aspects that even *you* don't understand.

Three Types of Entrepreneur

Inventors create a completely novel idea or invention. Such ideas or inventions are revolutionary. They're often called "disruptive technologies" because they displace whatever came before. They include products such as the copying machine, the web browser, and the cell phone.

Innovators take existing products, technology, or ideas and change them or apply them to new uses. Bringing a product like Teflon, which was developed for industrial use, to the consumer market, is an example of an innovation.

Introducers take an existing product and find a new market for it. The new market can be geographic, such as taking a product developed in Asia and introducing it in the United States, or demographic, such as taking a product designed for businesses and introducing it to consumers.

Return on Investment

Return on Investment (or ROI) is the financial gain angel investors receive for having invested in your company. You will hear investors refer to "ROI" repeatedly as you deal with them, so become familiar with the term and the concept.

ROI is the total amount of money owing to the investor as a result of helping fund your business venture. It is expressed in terms of an annual percentage—that is, the percentage of their investment earned each year of the investment (for example, a 30% ROI). This is calculated by dividing the amount of money investors make by the amount they invested, divided by the number of years it took to receive their gains.

You're a "good catch" if investors believe your business will provide them with a high ROI. The ROI that investing in your business offers has to be higher—much higher—than what an investor could obtain by putting their money into other, less risky investments, such as stocks, bonds, or real estate. Angel investors have to achieve a high return on investments in new ventures because such investing is risky. Some companies fail altogether and do not bring them any return. So their other investments have to balance those losses.

Investors realize their ROI from your company either when you have a "liquidity event"—such as selling the company to another company or selling stock on a public stock exchange—or at points that you've agreed upon in a different deal. For example, if your company is going to be very profitable and continue in business for a long time, you could make quarterly payments to the investor.

Angels will closely evaluate your business to determine the rate of ROI they are likely to receive.

2. The right market

Finding a business in the right kind of market is a critical consideration for angel investors. The quality of your business idea and the quality of your market are the number one elements they will evaluate when deciding whether to offer you funding. After all, you may have a great idea, but if the market for what you offer is relatively small (say, a business-to-consumer company serving only a local neighborhood or a niche business-to-business product), there's not going to be enough potential financial return to create a worthwhile investment for an angel.

Before sending money your way, angels will examine both your potential revenue and the size of your market. You will need to produce research and data to prove that this market actually exists—and to demonstrate that it is substantial and growing.

When a relatively large investment is being considered, the _total_ market size for your product typically needs to be at least as high as $50 million to $100 million per year. This would mean that if your company is able to capture 1% of a $100 million market, your annual sales would be $1 million.

A 1% market share may seem small, but it's realistic. Most investors will be wary if you predict a market share of more than 1% to 2% for your company's first year. And they won't expect higher than 5% in years three through five. Investors look favorably on entrepreneurs who under-promise and over-deliver.

Another way for your company to grow is for it to maintain a consistent market share in a growing market. A consistent 2% market share in a market growing at 50% per year fuels a company's growth at 50%.

The Market

Use the following worksheet to prepare a market analysis. You'll use this data when you answer a potential angel's questions about the size, characteristics, and potential of your market.

Where is your target market located? (City? Country? Region? Urban? Suburban?)

_____

_____

What are the characteristics of your target customer? (Consumer customers: Age? Income range? Gender? Family size? Education? Business customers: Number of years in business? Number of employees? Industry?)

_____

_____

_____

What motivates your customers to make purchases and what are their buying patterns?

_____

_____

_____

What is the size of your market?

_____

_____

What have the growth rates been in your market for the last 5 years?

_____

_____

What are the projected growth rates for the next 5 years?

_____

_____

What are some key trends in your market?

_____

_____

_____

The Competition

If you're meeting a genuine market need, there are—or will be—other companies who want a piece of the action. Investors want to see that you have a thorough understanding of the competition you face, both direct and indirect. Questions they'll ask:

- What differentiates you from the competition?

- What are the barriers to entry to your market? What's preventing other companies from doing exactly the same thing that you're doing?

- Who holds patents, trademarks, and/or copyrights?

- What are the start-up costs of other companies?

- How well funded is your competition? If there is a strong, well-funded competitor in your market, angel investors may shy away from funding you …

- … but angel investors will want to know who else is making money doing what you're doing. It can be reassuring to know that a successful model already exists in the marketplace. This helps show that there really is a market for your concept.

To gather this kind of information, go to local and business-school libraries, talk to vendors and suppliers in your industry, and do some sleuthing on the Internet to find out what your competitors are up to.

The Competition

Use the following worksheet to prepare a competitive analysis. You'll use this data when you answer a potential angel's questions about the size, characteristics, and strength of your competition.

What types of businesses (not specific companies) compete with you?

_____

_____

_____

Who are your specific competitors?

_____

_____

_____

What portion of the market does each competitor control?

_____

_____

_____

On what characteristics (price, quality, features) do you differ from your competitors?

_____

_____

_____

What are your competitive advantages?

_____

_____

Who will your future competitors be and what obstacles will they face as they try to enter the market?

_____

_____

_____

_____

QUICK**TIP**

Founderitis

Angels sometimes use the term *founderitis* to describe the inability of a CEO to be flexible and responsive to other's ideas and management. Founderitis is a red flag if an investor detects it when an entrepreneur is pitching for funds or during the negotiations. The remedy for this disease is to demonstrate that you're willing to take advice. This doesn't mean you're not running the show. (It's understood that an entrepreneur needs a healthy dose of ego to be successful.) It just means you know how to listen and take guidance from expert outsiders when needed.

3. A capable entrepreneur

There's a saying among investors that you should "bet on the jockey, not the horse" because it's the people, not the product or service, that make a successful business. Many investors say the first thing they turn to when reading a company's business plan is the section on the founder and the management team. They look for:

- **Personality.** Are you a stable and committed individual? Do you follow through on plans and actions you commit to? Do you get along well with team members and your investors? The best business enterprises work because of personal chemistry. Likewise, if you have a good relationship with potential investors, your chances of doing a deal with them are much higher.

- **Leadership.** Have you led teams successfully in the past? Are you CEO material or would your skills be better employed in another role in the company? Investors will assess whether you recognize when you need support and how you delegate responsibilities according to employees' and partners' skill sets.

- **Track record.** What is your past professional experience? What positions of responsibility have you held? What products have you successfully invented and brought to market? If you've already led a successful start-up venture or been part of a team that has, you have a distinct advantage.

- **Good communication skills.** You'll be in many situations where you'll be the one selling your business idea, your service, or your products. You must be able to explain your business idea clearly and briefly, with confidence. Do you communicate well with your team, your investors, and your customers?

- **Expertise in your field.** Are you a technical star? A brilliant marketer? An outstanding executive? Investors are looking for individuals who shine in their area of expertise. They expect you to be extremely capable already, not to have to learn on the job. Previous experience and past successes count for a lot.

Evaluate Yourself as an Entrepreneur

Use this worksheet to assess yourself as an entrepreneur. Highlight your talents by noting when you have demonstrated these attributes during your career. Then use these examples when you're presenting yourself and your ideas to potential investors.

Trait	Examples
Personality	
Leadership	
Track record	
Good communication skills	
Expertise in your field	

QUICK**TIP**

Get Smart (and Smarter) People on Board

Good leaders attract people who are as smart as—or smarter than—they are. This applies to team members as well as to outsiders who provide guidance, such as accountants and attorneys. Smart people make successful businesses—and investors recognize the ability to attract good people as a significant talent. The quality of the advisors you bring in goes a long way toward assuring investors that you know what you need to do to create a successful business.

4. A strong team

Investors are often asked, "Would you prefer an A team with a B product or a B team with an A product?" More often than not, the answer is they'd prefer an A team with a B product. The truth is that no matter how good the product or service, all businesses inevitably face hurdles. That's when an A team makes the difference between success and failure.

Many investors, particularly independent angels, base anywhere from 75% to 100% of their decision to invest on the quality of the team. Even the best idea will not create a viable and successful business without a quality team. Your ability to raise funds thus depends fundamentally on the strength of your management team. Investors want to know a great deal about who will be running the company and managing its key functions. They want to make sure these people are competent leaders. Investors look for proof that:

- The key leaders of the team are capable of running a company—not just producing a product or service—or that they are willing to bring in people who are.

- The members of the team responsible for key functions—technical, marketing, finance—are qualified. They must have the experience and expertise to get the job done well.

- Staffing levels are appropriate to achieve results.

- If your team is not complete, you understand your needs and future hiring requirements.

- You turn to qualified outsiders to fill in your knowledge gaps. Angels want to know if you've assembled a board of advisors or have hired competent attorneys and accountants.

Highlight the Skills of Your Management Team

Use this worksheet to record the highlights of your and your team's management skills and experience. (If the same person is performing more than one of these functions, break out their particular qualifications within each category.) Be sure to refer to this information when you discuss your company's management strengths with potential investors.

Function	Name	Experience, education, past successes
Day-to-day leadership of the company	AL	
Financial/Accounting	AC –	
R&D	∅	
Production	∅	
Marketing	AC	
Technology (Product related)	AC+	
Technology (Company related)		
Sales	→	
Fundraising	AC	
Investor relations	AC	
Business development	.	
Legal		

QUICK**TIP**

Write a Business Plan

A business plan outlines your entire business strategy, competition, market, financing, staffing, future developments, and the steps necessary to achieve your results.

If you do not have a business plan yet, it's time to develop one. The Planning Shop has two books to help you do this:

- *The Successful Business Plan: Secrets & Strategies*, and its accompanying Electronic Financial Worksheets, is recommended if you are seeking $10,000 or more, especially for a new business.

- *Business Plan In A Day*, which can also be used with the Electronic Financial Worksheets, is helpful for established businesses, especially those seeking less than $10,000.

Both books are available in bookstores throughout the U.S. and Canada, as well as from The Planning Shop at *www.planningshop.com*.

5. A killer business plan

"**S**end me your business plan." These are likely to be the first words you hear from a prospective angel investor. A strong business plan is your passport to investor funds. It is the one document that will be used to judge the quality of your idea, your market, your team. Without an impressive business plan, you won't be able to get past a first conversation.

Your business plan tells the story of your company by presenting your vision for the company's future and explaining how you will achieve it. The first parts of a business plan an angel will read are the executive summary and financial statements. Think of these two sections as an ad for the rest of the plan. They need to be concise, compelling, and irresistible to investors. Angels want to see immediately that you have a strong business idea, a large and growing market, and a solid grasp of financials. When they review your entire business plan, they're looking for the "secret sauce"—the key business ingredients no one has but you.

The critical components of your business plan:

- **Executive summary.** This is the single most compelling aspect of the entire document. It summarizes the key concepts of the whole business plan.

- **Company description.** This is the history, mission, and vision of your company. It includes the business model—in other words, how you (and hence your investor) will make money.

- **Product or service.** A clear, concise, one-page explanation of the product or service that your company offers.

- **Industry.** This section describes the health and growth of your industry. It shows that you have an understanding of the aspects of your industry that are key to your success.

- **Target market.** Identifies the types of people or businesses most likely to be your customers and explains their needs and wants. Details market size, growth, and trends. This is your chance to demonstrate how well you understand your customer and market.

- **Competition.** Evaluates other companies offering a similar product or service or filling a similar market need. Shows that you understand, and don't underestimate, the competition—and that you can explain market differentiators and barriers to entry.

- **Marketing and sales plan.** Sets out your strategy for reaching and selling to your customers. Indicates your distribution channels and pricing strategies.

- **Management team.** Describes the people in charge of key aspects of the company. Emphasizes past accomplishments and fit with job responsibilities.

- **Development plan, milestones, and exit strategy.** This section lays out the future of your business: your goals, how you plan to reach them, the milestones you are aiming for along the way, and your exit strategy. A viable exit strategy is one of the keys to attracting angel investors. They need to know how and when they will see a return on their investment before they offer their money.

- **Financials.** A set of financial statements showing the current financial status and future financial goals of your company for the next three years. Your financial statements should be in a professional format. They will demonstrate your ability to translate business operations and activities into financial realities and returns. Have an accountant review your financials, as most angels are financially savvy and will spot errors.

QUICK**TIP**

Restricted Stock

When angels invest in an early-stage company, they receive what's referred to as "restricted stock." When that company goes public, the holders of this kind of stock are restricted as to how much of their stock they may sell and when. This mechanism is put in place to prevent these investors from suddenly selling all their stock and depressing the stock price.

6. A profitable exit strategy

Angels invest in a business to get out. Generally, that's the time they receive a return on their investment. To make yourself an attractive possibility to an investor, start with the end in mind and consider what your *exit strategy* (also known as your *harvest strategy*) is going to be.

The three most common ways to make an exit are:

- **Sale.** This happens when your company develops and grows until it has a clear value and you sell it to an individual or group of individuals. Provided the sale meets or exceeds the targeted return, investors like this outcome because they receive straight cash.

- **Mergers and acquisitions (M&A).** In this case, your business grows and becomes a desirable merger or acquisition target. An acquisition happens when a larger company acquires your business, paying for it in cash or through an exchange of equity (stock) or a combination of the two. A merger occurs when you join forces with another company to make a larger entity. There is little cash involved in this scenario, as the investor will receive stock in the new company, not money. However, the expectation is that the whole will be greater than the sum of its parts, thus creating more potential return for your angel. Both outcomes are desirable for your investor if they do, in fact, provide the targeted return.

- **Initial Public Offering (IPO).** An IPO takes place when you publicly sell stock in your company for the first time. IPOs can provide you with a large amount of capital to continue to grow your business because the majority of the proceeds flow directly back to your company. Investors like IPOs because it converts their equity in your company into stock that they can eventually sell on the public market.

Who Might Buy My Company?

Gaze into the crystal ball and imagine what the future holds for your business. Who could buy it so that you and your investors reap the benefits of its success? Angel investors are very keen to hear that Company X or Company Y may be interested in buying your business down the line. Use this worksheet to speculate about possibilities.

List the major companies in your industry:

_____

_____

_____

_____

List any of these companies that have a history of acquisitions. Which companies have they acquired and how much have they paid for them?

_____

_____

_____

_____

Does your product or service meet a need within any of these companies? If yes, how does it meet that need?

_____

_____

_____

_____

Think of other companies not in this industry. Do any of them have a desire to enter this particular industry? Make a note of why these companies might be interested in your enterprise. List any businesses they've acquired and how much they've paid for them.

_____

_____

_____

_____

The Right Documents

Working with an angel investor means you no longer run your company alone. Before you enter into this partnership, making sure your business is in order both legally and financially prevents unexpected and potentially unpleasant surprises. Depending on what stage your company is in, these are some of the things you need to check, to make sure your company is in good shape:

Financials

- Forecast income statement, cash flow, and balance sheet
- Current profit/loss and cash flow
- List of any major accounts receivable
- List of any outstanding loans or major debts/accounts payable
- List of assets

Legal

- Corporate structure—that is, incorporation, LLC, or sole proprietorship
- Ownership: list of all current shareholders or those with ownership interest
- Promised equity, including any to current or former employees
- Contracts
- Regulatory compliance

Intellectual Property

- Intellectual property protection received to date: patents, trademarks, copyrights
- Pending IP filings
- Agreements with employees and third parties (including "work for hire" contracts)
- Ownership of core technology
- Licenses to use others' technology

Employees

- Compensation table
- Key personnel/functions
- Equity awarded/promised
- Stock option plan

Advisors

- Board of directors
- Advisory committee
- Key outside consultants—attorneys, accountants

Get Professional Help

If the documents checklist on this page looks daunting—and even if it doesn't—consider getting professional assistance to help you sort through the paperwork that you need. Lawyers and accountants can help ensure your finances and legal matters are in good shape.

4

Accomplishments

In this Step you'll:

☐ 1. Learn how to approach individual angel investors

☐ 2. Learn how to apply to angel groups

☐ 3. Discover what information to collect before your presentation

☐ 4. Learn what to present and how to present it

☐ 5. Find out what angels ask during presentations—and how to answer

☐ 6. Learn how to ask for money

☐ 7. Learn what to do after the presentation

Time-Saving Tools

You'll complete this Step more quickly if you have any of the following handy:

☐ A list of solo angels and angel groups to approach

☐ Your business plan

☐ Your executive summary

☐ Your financial statements

☐ Résumés and biographies for your management team

☐ Handouts to distribute at your presentation

☐ Answers to questions about your business

Step 4:
The Pitch

You've found an angel investor or angel group. You've focused your business concept, gathered compelling statistics about your market, rounded out your team, and polished your business plan. You're ready and eager to sit down and show an angel that your business is perfect for them.

Here comes the really big step—actually contacting the angel investor or angel investor group. And then, once you've contacted them, crafting a presentation that will convince them that they want to learn even more.

In this Step, you'll learn exactly what to say in your email or phone message when contacting an angel for the first time. You'll also learn how others can help you get that all-important first meeting with an angel. Then you'll learn what to say in your face-to-face pitch or presentation and which factors are the most critical to investors. And you'll find tips on how to make sure your presentation holds the attention and interest of your audience.

You'll also learn what *not* to include in your presentation. Investors look for red flags that will turn them off potential investments. Understand what these are so you can avoid touching a hot button.

With proper preparation, even a shy entrepreneur can contact a potential angel and make a winning presentation.

QUICK**TIP**

Save the Best for Last

Over time, your pitch and presentation will improve. You'll become more confident and you'll learn which questions to anticipate. That's why, if possible, you should try to schedule your very first meetings with the prospective angels who are lowest on your target list. Get some real-life practice before you present your pitch to your very best prospects.

QUICK**TIP**

Get to Know the Assistant

Assistants often control access to angel investors by screening phone calls and emails and setting appointments. If you don't have a referral source to an angel, call the angel's office and ask for the name and phone number of their assistant. Politely explaining your mission to an assistant can often bring better results than a cold call. Make the assistant your ally!

1. Contact an individual angel

The aim of contacting an individual angel is to get a face-to-face meeting so you can pitch your business idea in person. You'll get a much better hearing if you have met someone personally than if you are limited to a phone conversation or an email exchange.

The very best way to approach an individual angel investor is through someone they know. You're much more likely to get an angel investor to agree to meet with you if the request comes from one of their peers. If possible, see if your referral source will set up a face-to-face meeting with the potential angel investor for you (perhaps accompanying you to the meeting). Or at least ask your referring source, or their assistant, if they could make a first phone call or send an email to let the angel know that you'll be contacting them. That phone call would go something like: *"Hi, Mr. Chin. I'm John Carlisle's assistant and he's given Chris Lopez your name and number. John thinks you'd be interested in Chris's new business and hopes that the two of you can meet."*

You are much more likely to get a positive reception when you use the name of someone the angel knows and, ideally, respects. So if you have a personal reference, *always* obtain permission to use their name when contacting an angel investor. Include it in the subject line of your first email so your correspondence won't be deleted as spam.

Start by sending the potential investor an email with the executive summary of your business plan attached. State that you will follow up with a phone call to set up a meeting. If you do not know anyone in common, indicate in your email how you found their name (for example, *"I found your name and contact information through the Entrepreneurs' Forum"*).

Follow up your email with a phone call within three days. If you do not reach the potential investor, leave a polite voice mail, stating that you are following up on the email you sent, mentioning the name of the person who referred you and telling the potential angel that you will call again in a few days. Leave your contact information. If you do reach the investor, do not be surprised if he or she has not opened or seen your email. Offer to send it again and try to set up a time for a personal meeting.

QUICK**TIP**

Email Etiquette

Your initial email to a potential investor makes an important first impression, giving them insight into your communication skills and how well you can pitch your idea and get people's attention. Capital letters or exclamation marks in an email subject line are a fast track to the spam folder. Grammar and spelling matter, so run your emails through a checker. Even better, have someone else proofread them. Save sentence fragments, ellipses (…), and technical jargon for more casual correspondence.

Email Script: Your First Approach to an Angel Investor

From: *Your Name*

To: *Potential Angel's Name*

Subject line: *Howard Princeton* suggested I contact you regarding my company

[**Or:** Referred to you by the Entrepreneurs' Forum]

Dear *Potential Angel,*

A mutual acquaintance of ours, *Howard Princeton,* suggested I contact you. He thought you might be interested in learning more about my new company, *name of company,* and hoped that we would have a chance to meet.

[**Or:** I came across your name through the Entrepreneurs' Forum as someone who has an interest in investing in early-stage companies in the *type of* industry. I thought you would be interested in this investment opportunity because: *specific reason they might invest, such as their previous investments in similar companies, their expertise in your field, your company's growth potential.*]

The product/service we offer is: *describe this product or service in no more than two or three sentences.*

I have *number of* years of experience in *brief statement about yourself.* I have assembled a top-rate team with the skills and professionalism necessary to move this venture forward.

Attached is a brief summary of our business plan. I will follow up with you in the next few days to see if we can set up a time to meet. If you would like to contact me to discuss this opportunity further, please call me at *your phone number.*

Thank you for your time and consideration, and I look forward to talking with you further.

Sincerely,

Your Name, Your company's name

Your contact information

Attached: Executive Summary

Telephone Script: Your First Approach to an Angel Investor

Hello, *Potential Angel's Name. Howard Princeton* suggested that I should call you. My name is *Your Name* and I am the founder/president of *your company's name,* a start-up in the *name of* industry.

[**Or:** I came across your name *where/how* as having an interest in investing in early-stage companies.]

The product/service we offer is: *describe the product or service in no more than two or three sentences.*

I have *number of* years of experience in *brief statement about yourself,* and with a team of talented individuals, have started an exciting new company.

I'd like to take a few moments of your time to meet with you to better describe the business and the opportunity. *Set up an appointment.*

[**If you're leaving a message:** I'll call you back in a few days, or please call me at your earliest convenience at *your phone number.* Thank you, and I look forward to meeting with you.]

If you do not hear back in three days, call again:

Hello, *Potential Angel's Name.* My name is *Your Name,* and I am the founder/president of *your company's name. Howard Princeton* suggested that I might give you a call.

[**Or:** I came across your name *when/how* as having an interest in investing in early-stage companies.]

I phoned your office a few days ago to see if you might have an interest in investing in my company.

I had not heard back from you, so I thought I'd try again. I am sure you can recognize the enthusiasm and passion I have for my business. I believe this is an excellent investment opportunity for you because: *briefly give reasons why this is a good opportunity for the investor.*

Please give me a call back at your earliest convenience at *your phone number.* I hope to hear from you soon. Thank you. Goodbye.

If you don't hear back in a week, and you feel comfortable asking your contact to send the angel an email, do so. If not, phone again or send another email yourself. If after the third call or email, you haven't heard anything, move on. But you can recontact this potential angel again in a month or so. They may have been traveling or very busy at the time you originally contacted them.

2. Apply to an angel group

Angel groups are likely to have a structured application process. They will typically spell out their procedures and requirements on their websites, along with the industries and stages of investment they are interested in. If this information is not on their website, contact the angel group; they likely have documents detailing the application process, which they can send you by email or postal mail.

Thoroughly review the group's requirements. Typically, you'll need to submit an application form and/or the executive summary of your business plan. Some groups accept unsolicited applications, while others require a referral from a member of the group. Other groups may require you to pay an application fee.

Some angel groups ask for other documents, as well. These could include:

● Application form

● Executive summary of your business plan

● Complete business plan

● Financial statements (income statement, cash flow, balance sheet)

● Résumés of founders

● Letters of recommendation from angel group members

● Letters of recommendation from industry or business community leaders

Follow the angel group's process *exactly*. You do not want to be eliminated from consideration because you forgot to include something as easy to prepare as your résumé.

The Screening Process

Every angel group has slightly different screening procedures. Typically, these depend on the size of the group, whether or not they have paid staff, the sophistication of the angels, the number of applications they receive, and their clout in the funding market.

Most angel group screening procedures follow these steps:

- **Application.** Submit your application according to the angel group's requirements.

- **Pre-screening.** The angel group's staff or a committee of members or a designated member of the group (depending on the size and organization of the group) reviews your application to make sure it meets the group's general requirements. Applications that are incomplete, that do not fall within the group's investment criteria, or otherwise don't qualify for consideration will be declined or sent back for more information. Expect the pre-screening process to take 1 to 2 weeks.

- **Screening.** If your application is accepted for review, the angel group will ask for a complete business plan, including financial statements (if they have not done so already). Your business plan will be reviewed in depth. Some groups hold small meetings with the entrepreneur during this stage. According to the Angel Capital Education Foundation (ACEF), 10%–25% of entrepreneurs who apply to an angel group reach this stage. Expect this portion of the screening process to take another 1 to 3 weeks.

- **Presentation meeting.** If you pass the screening process, you're likely to be invited to make a presentation—your pitch—at a meeting of the angel group. Angel groups hold presentation meetings every 1 to 2 months.

QUICK**TIP**

Skin in the Game

Angel investors like it when entrepreneurs have "skin in the game"—in other words, when they've invested their own money (actual cash) in their business. Risking your own funds shows real commitment and a belief that you can succeed. Put another way, if you don't invest in your own company, why should they?

Angel groups generally require entrepreneurs to submit the executive summary of their business plan or a complete business plan. In addition, they may require the entrepreneur to complete an application form. Angel group application forms vary, but they contain common elements. The sample angel group application form on page 70 represents the typical type of information you'll need to supply.

Application Fees

Some angel groups charge an application fee ranging from $150 to $1,000. Find out what the fee is for. It may simply be to offset the administrative expenses an angel group incurs or it may be a way of ensuring that only serious entrepreneurs apply. In some cases, a fee could cover the cost of a mentoring component such as pre-presentation assistance, where members of the group coach you through a mock presentation before you present to the entire group. If you've never pitched investors before, getting coaching like this is money well spent. Before paying any fees, carefully read the group's investment criteria on their website, and make certain you're a good fit. If the fee is very high, make certain the group is legitimate—that is, that they are actually making many investments in start-ups each year.

Sample Angel Group Application Form

To have your business venture considered by Acme Angels, send this application with a check for the $200 non-refundable application fee. Then send your Executive Summary by email to acme_angels@acme_angels.com.

Company name:
_____

Contact name and title:
_____

Address:
_____
_____

Phone :
_____

Email:
_____

Industry (for example, enterprise software, Internet service, medical equipment):
_____
_____

Nature of product or service (100 words or less):
_____
_____

Year business started:
_____

Where business is located:
_____

Funding round (Seed? Series A? Series B?):
_____

Amount of funding being requested in this round:
_____

Proposed use of funds (100 words or less):
_____
_____

Dollar amount invested to date (from you and other investors):
_____

Key investors to date:
_____

Projected revenue in year 3:
_____

Prior 12-month sales/revenues:
_____

Most recent (3-month) sales/revenues:
_____

Who referred you to this group:
_____

In five words or less, explain why an investor should invest in your company (for example, original product, large market size, investor returns):
_____
_____
_____

3. Prepare for the presentation

Congratulations—an angel investor is interested in meeting with you to learn more about your company, or you've passed the initial screening phase of an angel group and you have the chance to pitch your idea in a face-to-face meeting or in front of a group. Now what? Prepare, prepare, prepare.

Your first step will be to learn as much as you can about the logistical details of your meeting or presentation. This information will be relatively easy to obtain if you're meeting with an angel group. However, you may or may not be able to get all these details from an individual angel.

- **Audience.** Find out who will be at the meeting or presentation. An individual angel may be alone or accompanied by their spouse, business associate, accountant, attorney, or another angel. An angel group will include all or several of its members. If you can, ask for the names of everyone who will be present and research their backgrounds before your presentation.

- **Format.** Check on the presentation format requirements. Many angel groups invite several entrepreneurs to present at the same meeting and have a structured format consisting of a 10–15 minute PowerPoint presentation, followed by a 10–15 minute Q&A session. This may lead to breakout discussions, where interested angels can meet one-on-one with entrepreneurs. If you're meeting with an individual angel, try to find out how much time they have set aside to meet with you.

- **Personnel.** Ask who from your team is expected to attend. Angel groups may have particular requirements. They will want to meet the CEO and/or founder and may want to meet other key members of your team, such as your top technology or marketing officer.

- **Location and setting.** Where will the presentation take place? It could be in a boardroom or hotel room if you're presenting to a large angel group or over a cappuccino at the local coffee shop or in a home or office if you are meeting with an individual angel.

- **Equipment.** Find out what type of presentation equipment, Internet connections, and electrical outlets are available at the presentation location. If the group has a projector, ask if you can take your laptop in the day before and hook it up to their equipment to check that everything works correctly. If presenting one-on-one to an individual angel, you may want to give the presentation on your laptop. Take an extension cord and your battery pack as a backup energy supply.

Presentation Day Checklist

Use this worksheet to help you assemble everything you need—and make sure you remember to take all of it with you on presentation day.

Date and time of presentation:

Departure time (with a significant cushion for delays built in):

Names of team members attending:

Location of presentation, map, and directions:

Phone number at location:

Office number of the angel:

Cell phone number of the angel:

Names of other attendees and any background information on them:

☐ Laptop

☐ Power cords and/or extra battery

☐ Projector (if necessary)

☐ Extension cord

☐ Handouts for your presentation (one for each attendee, plus extra copies)

☐ Copies of your business plan

☐ Additional support documentation (graphs, charts, reports)

☐ Business cards

☐ Actual product, beta version, demo

☐ Presentation on multiple disk forms (flash drive, CD, 3.5)

☐ Business-appropriate outfit

4. Make the presentation

To make your presentation a success, you'll need to polish and prepare in these three key areas:

- **Content.** Understand the critical points that you must cover. What do investors most want to know? What aspects of your content will be compelling to an investor? What should you *not* discuss in your limited time? What do you want the investor to remember? What do you want the investor to do when they have finished hearing your presentation?

- **Organization.** The content of your presentation must flow in a logical, engaging manner. Organize it so that you have sufficient time to cover your most important information. Make your most vital points at the beginning and end of your presentation—when they are most likely to be remembered.

- **Delivery.** To keep the attention of your audience, you must work on *how* you deliver your presentation, as well as its content. Delivery includes speaking style, opening remarks, body language, the quality of your PowerPoint slides, and how you handle questions.

QUICKTIP

Be Up to the Minute

Markets change constantly, and you want to make sure you have current information, especially if you are presenting to angels who are knowledgeable about your industry. Tracking current market information in your industry impresses angels. Update your business with the latest data available the day before you present.

Content

Think of your first pitch to an angel or angel group as a first date. You'll want to make a great first impression so they'll be interested in seeing you again. Share enough about yourself and your company to get their attention, but don't tell them everything. After all, if things go well, you'll have other chances to get to know one another better.

So how do you make a good impression on a prospective angel? Raise the issues that are most important to them:

- **Your business concept.** The nature of the product or service itself.

- **What need it meets.** There's got to be a real need or desire for this product or service if there is going to be a viable market.

- **The customer.** Investors have to be able to picture a real customer and understand why that customer would buy.

- **The size of the opportunity.** Generally, this means the size of the potential market for the product and how much market share your business is likely to secure.

- **The quality of the people who are on the team.** Do you and your team have the ability to turn an idea into a successful, high-growth company? Have you ever done it before? Can you deliver on your vision?

- **How much money they'll make, when they'll make it, and how they'll get their investment out.** What's the exit strategy? Who are likely acquirers if the exit will be an acquisition? How much money is the company likely to be worth? Within what timeframe?

Twelve Key Slides

Many angel groups require a PowerPoint presentation. Even if your angels don't demand this, a PowerPoint presentation will make you look focused and professional. Keep your presentation to a maximum of 12 slides, and make sure they cover this critical information:

1. Your company's name, a short company description, name of presenter(s).

2. The key points you want your audience to remember. They could include:

   - The competitive advantage your company offers

   - The size of the market

   - The growth potential of your company

   - Past successes of your management team

3. A description of your product or service. This might also include a picture, a video, or a demonstration.

4. Your specific target customers: who they are and the customer need that will be met by your product.

5. The market size: numbers and dollars, past growth, growth forecasts.

6. The competition: division of market share, how your product compares to theirs, your value proposition in comparison to the competition's.

7. Your team: who they are, past successes and experience, and why they are qualified to do the job.

8. The business model: how you will distribute your product, pricing strategies, how you will reach your customers.

9. The timeline: when you expect to reach key milestones.

10. Financials: a brief summary of key points from your income statement, balance sheet, and/or cash flow projections.

11. How much you are asking for in this round, how many future rounds are expected and how much you will request during those rounds, and how the funds will be used.

12. The investment opportunity: potential exit strategies and financial return for investors.

QUICK**TIP**

Handouts

Create handouts containing information you won't be addressing or that directly complements your presentation. Depending on your business, these could include:

- Your complete business plan

- Your financial statements (if not previously distributed or included in your business plan)

- Marketing materials

- Positive press coverage

- Letters of intent and/or contracts

- Photos or illustrations, especially of your product

- Technical information

Organization

Information conveyed at the beginning or end of your presentation will be the most memorable to your listeners. So place your most important—and convincing—information at the opening or closing of your talk. Information from the middle of your presentation will make a lesser impression. If you have any less-than-compelling details that must be mentioned (perhaps the strength of the competition or a potential intellectual property conflict), sandwich them in between your more convincing content.

Your Opening Line

What you say first sets the tone for your entire presentation and helps the audience decide whether to listen to you.

Begin with a simple and gracious acknowledgment:

❝ *I'd like to first say thank you for giving me [and my team] an opportunity to tell you about [name of business]. Please allow me to introduce myself and my team members ...* ❞

The very next thing you say must grab their attention and interest. Go for the "wow" factor, focusing on the fundamental issue that makes it likely that your business will be a success. A factor like this could be the size of the market, the nature of the product, the problem your company is solving, or the fact that you started a successful company previously.

Your opening line could come in the form of a statement:

" *Lawn care is an $8 billion-a-year indus-try. Nearly 25 percent of American house-holds spend more than $5,000 a year on lawn care. And yet there's never been a nationally known brand name in lawn care service. We intend to change that.* "

Your opener could also come in the form of a question:

" *Did you know that lawn care is an $8 billion-a-year industry, with nearly 1 in 4 American households spending over $5,000 a year on lawn care service? That's a huge market, yet there's never been a nationally known brand name in lawn care service. That's an opening in the market we intend to exploit.* "

What *Not* to Say

Investors often believe that company founders are too much in love with their product or service. By this, they mean that the founders are focused on the technical aspects of their product or service, rather than fully understanding the business realities. You'll want to be enthusiastic about your innovations or processes but also demonstrate that you have a clear grasp of the business itself—the strength of the competition, the market challenges—and a firm understanding of financial realities. So don't go into the nitty-gritty technical details of your product unless you are specifically asked to do so.

Weight of presentation components

PRESENTATION COMPONENT	WHAT IT IS	KEYS TO SUCCESS	PROPORTION OF WHOLE PRESENTATION
Product description	Your product or service described simply and briefly	Be succinct; avoid buzzwords and avoid being over-technical	10%–15%
Your team	Brief description of your team members' qualifications	Highlight previous experience, especially other successful start-ups	5%–10%
Market analysis and target customer	Data on your market and who you expect will buy your product or service	Be believable; use third-party sources to validate your data	10%–15%
Competitive analysis and value proposition	Description of the competition and their strengths; explanation of how the market share is divided and why you will be able to compete successfully	Beware of indicating that your competition doesn't exist or is weaker than it actually is	10%–15%
Business model	How your business makes money	Make sure you understand the basics of your industry, especially pricing and distribution	5%

PRESENTATION COMPONENT	WHAT IT IS	KEYS TO SUCCESS	PROPORTION OF WHOLE PRESENTATION
Financials	A summary of key aspects of your financial statements	These are difficult to convey succinctly; have full financials as a handout	5%–10%
Funding	Description of how much money is needed; any money raised to date; how many rounds of financing are expected; how funds will be used	Present realistic expectations of amount of money to be raised and number of funding rounds necessary	10%
Timeline	An illustration of quantitative and qualitative events	Present realistic estimates of time required to accomplish business goals	5%
Risk analysis	A very brief description of threats and risks to your success	Acknowledge significant risks, but keep this section short	Less than 5%
Potential return on investment (ROI)	Exit strategies; potential acquirers; potential total revenue	Show how revenues and ROI will develop over a number of years	5%–10%

Red Flags
for Investors

Experienced investors look for warning signs that an entrepreneur doesn't fully understand the nature of a business. The most common red flags:

- Stating that you have no competition or dismissing the competition too easily. Investors know that there's *always* competition.

- Inability to clearly and succinctly explain your product or service. If investors can't easily grasp the concept, they'll be turned off.

- Unrealistic expectations of your projected market share. It's not conceivable that you will gain much more than a few percentage points of a market, especially in the first years of business.

- Unclear or unbelievable business model. Investors look for proven distribution channels and revenue models.

- Pie-in-the-sky valuations. This shows you have an unrealistic sense of the marketplace and indicates you may be difficult to deal with in the future.

- Founder's unwillingness to give up a reasonable percentage of ownership. Once again, this indicates that you may be both unsophisticated and difficult to deal with.

- Plans to use investor funds to pay off past business or personal debt. Investors want their funds to be used for growth.

- Payments to finders for introducing you to investors. Again, angels want their funds to be used for company growth.

- Too many small, early investors. If you have a complicated current ownership or stock structure, it may make deals more complex than investors are willing to bother with.

- Believing you can grow your company to a very substantial size with only one round of financing.

- Projections for major growth involving a company that's been in existence for many years with the same management team. Investors won't find it believable that an existing company will experience major growth without major changes in strategy, as well as management.

- Misrepresentation. Once an investor has lost faith in your honesty, the game is over. Disclose any skeletons in the closet, such as previous business failures, bankruptcies, or legal disputes with former employers.

QUICK**TIP**

Practice, Practice, Practice

The single best way to improve your delivery is to practice your presentation many times before you give it to an angel, even if you are only going to a one-on-one meeting. Practice with business colleagues and advisors. Have them give you feedback and ask you questions. If you're going to be presenting in front of a large angel group, you may want to videotape yourself giving a practice presentation. Make sure you can finish your pitch in the prescribed period of time and are prepared for questions. The more you practice, the more comfortable and energetic you'll be when you actually give your pitch to the prospective investor.

Delivery

The key components of great presentation delivery are:

- **Professionalism.** Be well rehearsed. Stick to the key concepts of your presentation. Don't use slang or foul language. Keep humor to a minimum. You want your personality to shine through, but investors are judging you, as well as your company, and a difference in sense of humor could alienate your listeners.

- **Enthusiasm and energy.** Avoid speaking in a monotone. It's normal to be a bit nervous, and this can result in monotonous presentation. But angels want to see that you are genuinely excited about your company.

- **Compelling content.** Keep your ideas succinct. Don't go on at length about each aspect of your presentation. Give just enough to convey the essential information. Make your audience want more.

- **Responsiveness.** Allow investors to interrupt your presentation if they have questions. Listen carefully and respond as directly as you can. Even if you are the lead presenter, you can ask one of your team to answer a specific question if they are more qualified in a specific area.

- **Appearance.** People not only hear a presentation, they *see* the presenter. You must look professional and appropriate. If presenting to an angel group, it is appropriate to ask ahead of time about the expected attire for presenters (suits, dresses, sport coats, ties).

QUICK**TIP**

"I Don't Know"

When you're asked a factual question to which you don't know the answer, it's best to say, "I don't know, but I will look into that and get back to you." You can also turn this around by responding with something like, "I'm not exactly sure of that, but let me tell you what I do know ..." Never lie and never make anything up.

5. Prepare for Q&A

If they're at all interested in your business, prospective angels will ask you a lot of tough questions. Preparing for these is part of getting ready for your presentation.

Find an audience of experienced businesspeople and give them a practice presentation. (Ideally, the members of this audience should have investing experience.) Have these listeners grill you after you speak. Tell them to be as rough as possible. You want to be ready to handle the worst.

Angels will ask you probing questions about any weaknesses they perceive in your business, so you need to assess those weaknesses before you meet them. Be brutally honest in identifying potential problem areas. Then plan how you'll handle questions about your weaknesses. Sometimes potential investors will ask particularly aggressive or negative questions just to see how well you will respond. Handle each question thoughtfully and with respect. Try to respond to the question without becoming defensive or antagonistic.

On pages 83-85, you'll find a list of some of the questions prospective investors most commonly ask. Write down your answers to prepare yourself.

Questions Angel Investors Will Ask/Your Answers

Why do you think people will buy your product/service?

_____

_____

_____

I don't find the size and growth of your market believable. How do you know the market is truly that size?

_____

_____

_____

What evidence do you have that you will be able to capture that percentage of market share?

_____

_____

_____

How did you work out your valuation?

_____

_____

_____

What is the most compelling aspect of your business?

_____

_____

_____

If this is such a good idea, why hasn't it been done before?

_____

_____

_____

Why should I invest in your business?

_____

_____

_____

Questions Angel Investors Will Ask/Your Answers (continued)

Why do you think I would be a good investor for you?

_____

_____

_____

What will you do if you are not meeting or exceeding your financial projections?

_____

_____

_____

I think you've underestimated your expenses. How did you come up with these numbers?

_____

_____

_____

How will your competitors respond to you? How do you think you can stay ahead of better-funded and entrenched competition?

_____

_____

_____

What other start-ups are doing similar things in the same space? How and why will you beat them?

_____

_____

_____

What's going to keep a competitor from stealing your idea? Do you have any intellectual property protection in place?

_____

_____

_____

Can you explain your marketing strategy? Is it really affordable? Do-able?

_____

_____

_____

Can you provide greater detail regarding the production requirements for your product? How about other aspects of logistics and distribution?

_____

_____

_____

_____

Questions Angel Investors Will Ask/Your Answers *(continued)*

Who are the potential acquirers of your business when we're ready to exit? How much have they paid for other companies? What makes you think they'll buy yours?

_____

_____

_____

What in your past has prepared you to be CEO of a company like this?

_____

_____

_____

What weaknesses do you currently see in your management team?

_____

_____

_____

What other key management positions will you have to fill? Do you have anyone in mind? How much will they cost?

_____

_____

_____

Why don't you have any customers yet?

_____

_____

_____

Can you provide best, worst, and expected case scenarios for future funding needs?

_____

_____

_____

Tell me the status of your personal lives. What else is going on that will distract you from giving this company your complete attention?

_____

_____

_____

_____

_____

_____

_____

QUICK**TIP**

It's Not Over 'til It's Over

Very few deals are finalized on the day of the presentation according to the terms suggested by the entrepreneur. Most are completed after a period of negotiations between the parties. So at the end of your pitch, don't try to close the deal. Just ask the angel if the deal is "do-able." This will leave the door open for additional conversations and will allow the angel to explain any reservations they have, which you can then address.

6. Ask for the money

It's crunch time. You've made your presentation, explained your concept and your business model, introduced the team, and highlighted the great investment opportunity it all represents. Now ask for the money.

Making a pitch is like being in a traditional sales environment: if you don't ask for the sale, you won't get it. So make clear to a potential investor what your funding needs are. It's time to shine and to show pride and confidence in your venture and its ability to succeed.

Be direct and clear about the amount you are requesting and how you intend to use it. Highlight how the capital will allow your company to thrive. Then be prepared to be flexible. Even if angels are interested in investing, they may have a different sum in mind or suggest a different deal structure.

After your presentation, whether you are in the boardroom at the end of your pitch, having coffee with an individual angel, or speaking to angel group members in a breakout session, be persistent and follow up your pitch immediately. Ask the investors:

- Are you interested in my proposal?

- Is this a "do-able" deal?

If the answer is a qualified yes, as in "Possibly, but I need to think about it," follow up with other questions:

- What can we do to make this a deal?

- What did you like about our deal?

- How does it compare to other deals that you've looked at recently?

- Would additional information be of interest to you?

If the answer is a straight "No," ask

- What can we do to make this a do-able deal?

- What other suggestions might you have for us to improve this deal?

- Who else would you suggest we talk to?

End the conversation by expressing your gratitude and your appreciation for the angel or angel group's time and interest.

Before You Leave

Before leaving the meeting, ask the angel or angel group when they anticipate making a decision. Find a reason to follow up with them. Perhaps you were unable to answer one of their questions or you may want to expand on something you said or provide some additional information to the angel. Ask if there is any further information they would like from you and how they prefer to stay in touch—by phone, cell phone, or email? Collect business cards or contact information from each person in the room.

QUICK**TIP**

Will Angels Steal My Idea?

Most angel investors invest in businesses to make money, not to steal ideas. Professional investors, whether individuals or members of an angel group, will invest in the belief that you and your team are the most capable people to achieve the goals of the business. But as in every area of life, there are unscrupulous people out there. Before you present your business idea to a potential investor, make sure they are reputable by conducting a few background checks on them. Talk to others who know them and do a little due diligence (see page 38).

7. After the presentation

Send a handwritten thank you note or a personalized email to the angel or angel group within 24 hours of the presentation. Include:

- Your appreciation for their time

- Three or four key points for the investor to focus on

- Clarifications of any points you feel needed additional attention

- Responses to any inquiries that were left unanswered

- A closing that restates your appreciation and requests an opportunity to meet again

Handwritten Thank You Note

Dear *Potential Angel,*

Thank you for taking the time to meet with me *[us]* and allowing me *[us]* to share with you the investment potential in *name of company.*

We represent an outstanding opportunity in the marketplace. Our company will: *3 main points you want them to remember.*

I *[we]* appreciate that you hear of many investment opportunities, but I *[we]* strongly believe that our plan provides a compelling picture as to *name of company's* ability to meet its goals.

I *[we]* look forward to visiting with you again in the near future.

Sincerely,

Your name

Your contact information

Signatures of team members

Thank You Email

Dear *Potential Angel,*

I *[we]* would like to begin by expressing my *[our]* sincere gratitude for your taking the time to meet with me *[us]* and allowing me *[us]* to share with you the investment potential in *name of company.*

During our meeting, you raised a couple of points that we needed to clarify. *Include brief responses to any questions you were unable to respond to or points that needed further clarification. Limit this to 3 to 4 bullet points.*

I would like to reiterate the reasons why your investment in *name of company* would bring you benefits: *3 to 4 bullet points.*

Thank you for your interest in *name of company.* I *[we]* will be following up with you in the next few days to answer any additional questions you may have.

Sincerely,

Your name

Your contact information

Attachments (if including)

5

Accomplishments

In this Step you'll:

☐ 1. Learn how to determine how much money your company needs

☐ 2. Learn about the stages of investment

☐ 3. Understand valuation

☐ 4. Consider factors that affect your company's valuation

Time-Saving Tools

You'll complete this Step more quickly if you have any of the following handy:

☐ Cash flow and revenue projections for 1 to 3 years

☐ Anticipated funding needs

☐ Research on funding that other companies in your industry have received

Step 5:
Valuation

Valuation is one of the most critical things you'll negotiate with your investors. The valuation of your company determines how much your company is worth, how much money you'll be able to raise, and how much ownership of your company you'll keep. As well, the valuation you agree to at the outset will have a major impact on the valuation you will be able to set in the next round of financing—and even on whether you'll be able to raise another round.

A basic tenet of raising money is that early money is the most expensive. This means that, in the earliest stages of your company, you will give up the greatest amount of equity per dollar raised. Thus, you don't want to raise more money than you truly need—and give up more equity than you need to—in your first rounds of fundraising.

So first figure out how much funding your company truly needs at this stage. Recognize that you can raise more funds at the next stage of development. Then negotiate a fair (not an inflated) valuation.

QUICK**TIP**

No Blue Book for Companies

Valuation is an art, not a science. There's no completely objective way to measure what a company, especially a start-up business, is worth. There's no Kelley Blue Book price listing for businesses. So don't focus on a non-negotiable figure for your company's valuation just because a seemingly similar company was valued at that price. Instead, do everything you can to improve the perception (and the reality) that your company will be a winner—a big winner.

QUICK**TIP**

Cash Flow Statement Made Easy

An easy way to prepare financial statements is with The Planning Shop's Electronic Financial Worksheets. This MS Excel package of worksheets and financial statements streamlines the process of creating and formatting financial statements. Enter your financial figures once, and they'll automatically flow through to all the other relevant statements (Income Statement, Cash Flow Projections, and Balance Sheets). Order the Electronic Financial Worksheets online at *www. planningshop.com*.

1. Determine how much money you need

There is a direct correlation between how much money you raise each time you seek financing and how much equity you give up. The more money you raise, the more ownership you will be required to relinquish to your investors. So you don't want to raise more money than necessary.

On the other hand, raising money takes time away from running your business. So you don't want to raise less money than you need to take your company to the next level of development. It's clear that figuring out how much money to ask for is a critical step in the angel hunting and negotiation process.

Keep in mind that angel investors will frequently suggest you raise a different amount of money than you originally sought. They may feel you are overly ambitious and should raise less money until your concept is further developed. Or they may feel that you haven't asked for enough to provide you with the funds you need to reach your milestones.

Listen carefully to your angel investors, especially those experienced in your industry. A good angel investor will be on your side.

Cash, Cash, Cash

When you prepare your business plan, you will be doing financial projections for the next 3 to 5 years that focus on eventual profits. But your business won't be able to make all those future millions if it doesn't survive the early years before you are fully profitable.

So the most important financial statements you can prepare before you ask for money are the cash flow projections for the next 12 to 18 months and calculations of how much money you're likely to need for the next three years or so. Estimate your need for capital as accurately as possible to ensure that you ask for the right amount of money—enough to grow the business and not run out of cash.

A general rule is to *overestimate costs and underestimate income.* All businesses have unexpected expenses and unexpected setbacks. Even when growth goes faster than anticipated (a good problem to have!), you'll use up money more quickly than you imagined. Build in a generous cushion for error.

How much of the ownership of your company you'll give up depends on what stage your business is in when you receive funding. The chart on page 96 shows an example for a start-up business at various stages of development. The *bootstrapping* stage is when you are building your company with money from your own pocket, without any outside funding. The *seed* stage is before you are shipping product or making sales; this is when angels often begin to invest and you frequently do not set a valuation at this stage. Series A and B funding rounds generally occur after you've made some substantial progress (for instance, when you are already in production and then perhaps after you are already making sales).

Equity Ownership for a Start-up

STAGE	BOOTSTRAPPING	SEED	SERIES A ROUND	SERIES B ROUND
Money needed for	Business plan. Traveling to see competitors. Sourcing equipment.	Developing prototype. Hiring initial personnel. Initial marketing. Operations plan.	Fully functional operation. Hire key personnel. Marketing. Insurance.	Increase marketing. Expand staff. Increase production.
Amount of money raised	Minimal	$100,000	$350,000	$1 million
Source of money	Founders' personal savings, family & friends	Angel investors	Angel investors	Angel group members
% ownership given up in round	0%	To be determined	35%	40%
Founder's % ownership	100%	To be determined	65%	25%

Money Needed at Various Funding Stages

Fill out this worksheet to estimate how much money you'll need at various stages of your company's development, based on your financial projections. These numbers should help guide you when considering how to stage your funding rounds.

Stage of Development	Amount of Money Needed at This Stage	Potential Source	What the Money's For
Bootstrapping			
Seed			
Production (possibly Series A)			
Expansion (possibly Series B)			

Return on Investment (ROI)

Return on Investment (or ROI) refers to the total amount of money the investor gains in return for the money they put into your company. ROI is expressed as an annual percentage. It is calculated by dividing the total amount of money investors gain as a result of investing in your company by the amount they invested and then dividing again by the number of years their money has been in your business.

Let's say an angel invests $100,000 in a company and receives 20% of that company's equity in return. After three years, the company is sold for a profit of $1,000,000 (after accounting for all debts and outstanding expenses). The investor's share of the profit will be $200,000. So they will have seen a gain of $100,000 (remember: $100,000 of the $200,000 is their own money). That gain is then divided by the amount invested ($100,000 divided by $100,000), and then it's divided again by the three years of the investment. So the investor's ROI is 33.3%.

The basic factors determining an investment's ROI include:

- All financial investments and costs, including the initial investment and any follow-on investments

- All financial gains—including the proceeds of the sale of the company, the return of the investor's initial capital, and funds received as dividends or payments (if any)

- Time period—how long it has taken to realize these gains

Knowing an investment's potential ROI makes it easy for investors to compare different investment opportunities. They can compare likely ROIs from mutual funds, stocks, real estate, and investments in new companies.

Angel investors need to see a very high ROI on their investment in your company because they need to exceed the potential ROI from less risky investments. The average ROI for an angel investor in seed-stage companies is around 34%, but many of the companies angels invest in fail, producing no returns. As a result, angels depend on a few companies in their portfolio to provide them with extraordinarily high profits. Some investors set a specific ROI that they are trying to achieve, generally between 25% and 40% annually.

2. Stage the investment

You would be unlikely—and possibly unwise—to raise all the money you'll need at one time. Most entrepreneurs, especially heads of companies that will eventually be worth many millions of dollars, raise funds at different times in the development of their enterprise.

One reason to raise money at different stages in your development is that money raised when your company is more mature costs less in terms of how much equity, or portion of ownership, you have to give up in return. There's a reason for this: The further along you are in your company's development, the less risky the investment is for the angel. When your company is not much more than a good idea, or perhaps a prototype of a product, there are lots of risks. You may not actually be able to manufacture what you're developing, the costs may be higher than projected, and customers may not respond. Investors need to receive a premium return for taking a chance on such a risky endeavor.

With each stage of development—perfecting the product, securing paying customers, developing a significant portion of market share—the risk for the investor is reduced. Moreover, your company becomes worth more, or has a higher *valuation*, the more developed you are and the closer you are to profitability.

Thus, in later stages, it's likely you won't have to give up as much equity for each dollar you raise. For instance, for $100,000 of seed money, you might have to give up 40% of your company. But a year or two later, when your product has been eagerly received by an ever-expanding market, you might have to give up only 5% for that same $100,000.

QUICK**TIP**

Rounds

Money for your company is raised in *rounds*. Each round of funding is designed to finance a business through a specific period of development until the next funding stage is reached, until the company can be self-sustaining, or until it has an exit event (such as an initial public stock offering). Some angel investors invest in just one or two rounds of financing, while others have the financial resources and commitment to participate in several.

Financing Stages

Typically, entrepreneurs raise money for their companies, especially companies that grow to be valued at many millions of dollars, through a number of stages. Angel investors (and venture capitalists) expect investments to be staged over a number of years.

Keep in mind that you give up a portion of your own ownership of the company at *every* stage or funding round. For example, you might give up 35% of the equity after the seed round, leaving you with 65% ownership. Then you might give up another 30% after the first round, now leaving you with 35% ownership.

Funding stages include:

- **Seed money.** The first capital raised by a start-up company, typically from angel investors. Seed money provides the funds for the initial development of the company. You use it to create a prototype of your product, hire key members of the management team, rent space, find your first customers, and launch your first marketing efforts.

  Investors, of course, receive equity in the company in return for investing at the seed stage. If a valuation is determined, angels will receive stock. However, sometimes the investor and entrepreneur do not determine a valuation for the company at the seed stage, especially if subsequent rounds of financing are anticipated in the near future. Instead, the investors receive the right to have their equity converted to shares at the price, often with a premium added, set at the next round of financing.

While seed money can be expensive in terms of giving up more equity per dollar, obtaining seed financing can make the difference between being able to create a company and not being able to get off the ground at all.

● **Series A.** The first round after seed-stage financing is called Series A. At this point, you will definitely establish a valuation for the company (if you haven't already).

Typically, you will raise enough money in your Series A round of financing to cover your financing needs for the next 12 to 18 months or until you have enough income to be self-sustaining, whichever is earlier.

In return for their funds, investors will receive equity in the form of stock. Almost always, this equity is in the form of *convertible preferred stock*. Preferred stock gives the investors certain additional rights—or preferences—above those who hold *common stock*. Generally, these rights have to do with receiving dividends and being protected, in terms of being paid back first, in case the company goes under. The stock is *convertible* to common stock in case the company goes public.

You won't want to spend all your time raising money, so base your Series A financing needs on careful financial projections of how much money you will need for the next year or two.

QUICK**TIP**

Small Piece of a Big Pie?

When the reality of having to give up a piece of the ownership of "your" company sets in, you'll be faced with the question that many investors will ask: "Do you want to own a small piece of a big pie or a big piece of a small pie?" In other words, are you willing to give up a big piece of your company in order to create a much larger company? If you want your company to grow, your answer will be "Yes! I'll take a small piece of a big pie."

- **Series B and Series C.** Subsequent rounds of financing are referred to as Series B and Series C rounds. Because it takes time to raise money, many businesses start looking for Series B round investors a year after their Series A round, in order to find funds that will continue to fuel growth.

By this time (if not before), you may be looking for a substantial amount of money—in the range of many millions of dollars. This scale of funding is usually beyond the capabilities of most angels or even angel groups. So when you are at this stage, it may be time to seek funding from venture capitalists (see pages 15-18). This can potentially present conflicts with your angel investors in terms of protecting their rights and involvement. Some angels, however, have good relationships with VCs and can help you secure them.

However, if you agreed upon unusual terms in previous funding rounds with angel investors—perhaps ones that were overly protective of their rights or overly generous to you and other founders—your agreements may scare off future venture capitalists. That's another reason why it is important to have an experienced securities attorney take you through the legalities of every funding stage.

3. Understand valuation

In the course of negotiating a deal with an investor, you'll be discussing many things, including: what kinds of authority the investor will have (such as a seat on your board of directors), how they'll be protected if the company fails, and whether or not they are guaranteed the right to invest in future rounds.

But the single most important thing you'll be negotiating is the *valuation*, or worth, of the company. In other words, you'll be determining the price of the shares in your company that they will be buying. Once the angel has decided how much to invest, the valuation of your company will determine the percentage of ownership your angel will receive in return for their money.

Let's say an angel has decided to invest $100,000 in your company. If you agree that the valuation of your company is $1,000,000, the angel will have 10% ownership. If you instead agree that the valuation of your company is $500,000, the angel's investment will represent 20% ownership. And if you both agree that your company, at this early stage, is worth only $200,000, your angel will have 50% ownership of your company.

Get Real

When entering a negotiation, entrepreneurs (especially those who have never raised money before) and angels often have very different views of how to value a company and very different expectations of how much angels will receive in return for their money.

A novice entrepreneur might be thinking: *"I've got a killer idea that will blow the competition out of the water. My company is going to be worth $100 million within a few years. If an investor gives me $100,000 now, and I give them 10% of the company, they'll make $10 million. That's a great investment."*

Meanwhile, an experienced angel investor might be thinking: *"This is a good idea and it looks as if they have a capable management team. They have real potential. But I'm somewhat concerned about the competition and whether someone else will beat them to market. They'll need at least a few rounds of financing to get sufficient market share to be worth anything. My percent of equity will be reduced in each round. It's going to take at least five years before they're ready for an exit. If I put this money in another investment, such as real estate, I could get at least 15% to 20% interest a year with less risk. I need to get at least 40% of the company to make it worth my while."*

As you can see, the angel is considering many other factors besides the quality of the idea itself. Remember: For the angel this is an investment and a risky one at that. Angels need to realize a financial return that is significantly higher than the return they could get from other, more secure, alternatives. High risk means high rewards are needed. Here's the reality: You should expect to give up between 20% and 40% of the ownership of your company for a first-round (Series A) investment. If the percentage represented by the angel's investment is less than that, you have probably given your company an unrealistically high valuation. On the other hand, if you give up more than 20%–40%, you will not have enough equity for subsequent rounds and to give to key personnel.

Pre- and Post-Money Valuation

You will hear investors and entrepreneurs refer to two different types of valuation—pre-money and post-money:

- **Pre-money valuation** represents the value of the company immediately before any round of investment. Valuation is difficult to calculate if the company is a start-up or an early-stage company with little or no operating history or revenue. At this stage, the valuation is negotiated between you and your angel investors and is based on a variety of factors, including potential intellectual property assets, including patents, trademarks, and copyright; market size expectations; and the experience of your team, among other things. Pre-revenue start-ups rarely have pre-money valuations of more than $10 million and are typically valued at much less than that.

- **Post-money valuation** is the valuation of a company right after a given round of financing. The amount of investment and the shares given up for that investment determine the post-money valuation of a company. The valuation is calculated by adding together the agreed-upon pre-money valuation and the total cash invested during that round.

Say you've valued your already-operating eco-friendly garden products company, Lime Tree, at $2 million. This valuation is based on current sales, customer commitments, and projected revenues. You've now found angel investors who are going to invest $1.5 million in your company. The new, post-money valuation of your company will therefore be $3.5 million. The angel investors now own 42.8% of the equity of Lime Tree ($1.5 million is 42.8% of $3.5 million).

QUICK**TIP**

Send in the Accountants

If you're working with sophis-ticated angels or angel groups and are seeking an investment of more than $100,000, it's probably a good idea to hire an accountant to review your financials. Find someone who has worked with investors to advise you on what angels look for when they scrutinize financial statements. You want your financial documents to be professional and realistic.

High vs. Low Valuation

Most entrepreneurs set out looking for a high pre-money valuation, while investors prefer a lower pre-money valua-tion. A lower valuation means the founders will give up a higher percentage of ownership share of the company for a given angel investment level.

Although it sounds counterintuitive, a high valuation is not necessarily the best thing for you, even if you find an angel investor willing to provide funds based on that high valua-tion. The primary reasons are:

- A high valuation may scare off future investors.

- A high valuation may force a "down round" in the future. This is where your company is given a new, lower valu-ation in a future round of investing because it is seen to have been overvalued in an earlier round. (See page 107 for more.)

Many entrepreneurs make the mistake of thinking that their company should have a high pre-money valuation. They believe the valuation should be based only on the future potential value of their company—how much revenue they'll make, based on their current projections. But this is not the case. The value of your company is based on a *combination* of work achieved to date and the company's potential.

The more progress a company has made in its development, the more it is worth. What that means to you is that the more work you do in moving your company toward profit-ability, the more money you'll be able to raise. And, most importantly, the less percentage of ownership you'll give up for that money.

Dilution:
What It Is and How It Works

Early angel investors want to do everything they can to protect against the reduction—or dilution—of the value of their shares. Dilution occurs when a shareholder's ownership value is reduced in subsequent rounds of financing because the price of the new shares being sold is lower than the price the investor originally paid. (These are called *down rounds* because the value of the company, and the shares, has gone down.)

Let's say an investor paid $1 per share for 100,000 shares in an energy conservation company, and they received 40% of the equity. But in the next round of financing, the value of the company has decreased or the new investors have negotiated a far better deal. Those new investors are only paying $0.50 a share for 100,000 shares (still representing 40% of the company). That means the value of the original investor's 100,000 shares has gone from $100,000 to only $50,000—it's been *diluted*.

To protect against a dilution like this, investors commonly require anti-dilution provisions in the funding contract. These anti-dilution provisions entitle the earlier investors to receive additional shares in the company based on the new, lower price in any subsequent down rounds as a means of reducing the price they originally paid to the new price. In other words, the angel investors in that energy company would now receive an additional 100,000 shares—at no cost—to bring their effective purchase price to the same $0.50 as the investors in the second round. (They paid $100,000; the new price is now $0.50, so they are entitled to 200,000 shares at the new price. Since they only originally received 100,000 shares, they get an additional 100,000 now at no cost.)

You can see why early investors like and want these anti-dilution measures. You can also see why second round investors don't like the fact that the earlier round investors are now getting free stock. And, compounding all this, because these provisions result in only *protected investors* receiving free shares of stock, those who received stock in the first round who do *not* have protected shares (such as the company's founders and management—you!) usually have to reduce their percentage of ownership.

Anti-dilution provisions are common. So you'll want to minimize the impact they have on your company and on your ability to raise subsequent rounds of financing. There are ways to word these provisions so that they will have the least impact on your company. That's why it's important to consult with a knowledgeable securities attorney. And the best protection against anti-dilution is to work hard to increase the value of your company between rounds of financing, so that its value is continually increasing!

CK TIP

Save Something for the Help

Remember that you will probably have, or want, to give some equity (stock) to key employees, both to those already on board and as an incentive to those you wish to hire in the future. Agree with your investors on an amount of stock to set aside for these employees. Otherwise, their stock will have to come from your personal shares.

4. How much is your company worth?

The valuation of your business is the amount that you and your investor(s) agree your company is worth. It's a crucial, but not easy, number to reach. Calculating valuation is a fundamental part of your negotiation with angel investors. The number you agree upon determines how much ownership of the company you and your team will retain.

Valuation also has an impact on your ability to raise funds in the future. If you have too high a valuation, you may scare off future investors or be forced into *down rounds,* where the value of your company is decreased. Investors hate down rounds, and they create anti-dilution headaches.

If your valuation is too low, you will give up a higher percentage of your company's shares than you need to. Moreover, you will be left with too little equity to offer to additional key employees that you recruit later.

Most angels have an idea of what valuation they think is appropriate for your company. But valuation is a negotiation—you and your angel investor will debate this issue during the process of doing a deal.

The best way to prepare for this is to do research on the valuation of comparable companies. To find such information, check sources like Dow Jones Venture Wire (*http://venturewire. dowjones.com*). Also ask other entrepreneurs in your industry. Consult with business-school professors. Read local business newspapers for information about sales of companies. Compare your business only to companies in your geographic area and within a recent timeframe.

Valuation Factors

A variety of factors comes into play when determining a company's valuation. These include:

- Size of potential market

- Experience of the team

- Nature and viability of the business concept

- Extent of the competition

- Number and quality of potential acquirers

- Health of the Initial Public Offering (IPO) market

- Likely number of additional financing rounds required

- Quality and names of any committed customers

- Quality and names of any committed strategic partners

- Stage of company development

- Intellectual property protections

- Comparable price of other start-ups in the industry

- Amount of revenue to date, if any

Valuing a company that is little more than an idea and a basic business plan is very different from putting a value on a company that has been in operation for a year or two, is already shipping products, has customers, or has formed strategic partnerships.

You can increase the value of your company by moving forward in your development as far as you can prior to seeking financing. The more of the following factors that you have in place, the better will be your position at the negotiating table:

- High-quality, thoroughly researched business plan

- Believable, realistic financial projections

- Reliable data, identifying a large, reachable market

- Your own history of building, and selling, a successful company (a major plus!)

- Team members with successful experience in the industry

- Demonstrated commitment to your company through investment of your own funds

- Funds already raised by other committed investors

- Working prototype or beta product

- Positive press coverage

- Intellectual property protections in place (copyrights, patents, trademarks)

- Strategic partners committed, especially with brand-name companies

- Distribution agreements signed

- Product ready for production

- Product shipping

- Letters of intent from customers, especially brand-name companies

- Contracts with customers, especially brand-name companies

- Actual sales revenues

- Profits

Negotiation Strategies

Get an Attorney

By the time you begin negotiating your company's valuation with an angel, you must have an experienced securities attorney advising you. Every decision you make will have significant future ramifications, in terms of money, control, taxes, and many other factors. The few thousand dollars your attorney charges could save you a few million if your company is a success. Your lawyer can also be the "bad cop" during negotiations.

Be Prepared

Before negotiations begin, determine your investor's goals and assumptions: what level of ROI they want to achieve, how long they expect to hold the investment, and what percentage growth they believe is realistic. If possible, talk to someone else the investor has negotiated with to get an idea of their negotiating style and hot buttons.

Try to establish comparable valuations. Do your homework about what similar companies in the same industry and at the same stage of development as yours received as valuation.

Know What's Most Important to You

Before you begin negotiations, discuss with your attorney the provisions that are going to have the most impact on you both financially and in terms of running the business. This will allow you to give in on provisions that are not as critical and to hang tougher on those that truly matter.

At the start of negotiations, look for areas of agreement, so you don't begin in an adversarial position. Remain flexible; if you enter discussions with non-negotiable issues, you'll already have backed yourself into a corner, lessening the possibility of completing a successful deal.

Remember: You want the investor to respect you as a negotiator who is reasonable and realistic. If you're too stubborn, antagonistic, or arrogant, they'll think you don't have the personality to run a company.

Lower Perceived Risk

To an investor, there's a direct correlation between risk and reward: The higher the risk, the higher the reward has to be. Anything you can do before you seek funding that lowers perceived risk—such as having key customers lined up, a prototype tested, or key employees in place—increases the value you'll receive.

The Best Time to Negotiate Valuation

Try to delay valuation discussions until your investors have had time to become enthusiastic about the prospects of your business, the size of the market, and your ability to build a successful company. Disagreeing about valuation early in the process makes it less likely that an investor will have an open mind when they are examining the business itself.

Your investor, especially if they're sophisticated, will begin to probe at your negotiating position early, perhaps at your first meeting. This initial probing won't necessarily take the form of hard questions such as "How much do you think this company can be valued at?" or "How much equity do you want?" Rather, your angel may make softer queries such as "How big is the market going to be and what percentage of market share do you think you'll gain?" or "What do you think this company will be worth five years from now?" The answers to those questions will form the structure on which they'll be judging the value of the company.

In general, the investor is going to expect you to be the first to mention a number. Remember: The lowest number you mention is the highest number you'll ever receive.

6

Accomplishments

In this Step you'll:

☐ 1. Learn what is included on a term sheet

☐ 2. Understand the negotiation process

☐ 3. Learn how contracts are created and signed

☐ 4. Learn how the investment money is delivered

Time-Saving Tools

You'll complete this Step more quickly if you have any of the following handy:

☐ An experienced securities attorney

☐ An accountant

Step 6:
The Term Sheet

You will first do verbal negotiations with your angel about the major aspects of your deal. These aspects include the valuation of the company, the percentage of equity the angel will own, the percentage of equity set aside for future employees, the percentage of equity you'll own, and what type of participation your investors will have on the board of directors.

Then it's time to put all of this in writing. In some cases, especially when raising relatively small amounts of money, you'll go right to the contract stage. With more sophisticated angels, you may be given a *term sheet*.

A term sheet is a non-binding document that summarizes all the terms you and your investor negotiated. In effect, it is the offer the angel is making to you. The term sheet will include items such as the valuation you've agreed to and the equity your investor will receive.

Sophisticated angels and members of angel groups will probably have the term sheet drafted by lawyers. Your angel will fill in the blanks with the numbers you agree upon in your negotiations.

QUICK**TIP**

Straight to the Contract

Experienced angels usually have their lawyers draft a term sheet. If you are dealing with an inexperienced angel who is dependent on you to find an attorney, you may want to go straight to a contract instead. (Whether or not you go straight to contract, you will need an experienced securities attorney on *your* team.)

Over the years, as angel investing has become more sophisticated, term sheets have become more complex and more detailed. They will include the terms investors want that may not have been mentioned in your oral discussions, such as anti-dilution provisions (see page 107). This range of terms reflects the increasing diversity in ways investors choose to structure their participation in the investment (such as through buyouts and bridge financing) and the variety of investment securities they opt for, including debt, equity, hybrids, and warrants.

This process is complicated. You will need an experienced attorney to assist you. You may need an accountant as well. And you'll need patience and flexibility because the process takes time. You'll want to make sure you protect your rights and interests, but you don't want the angel to decide you're impossible to work with and walk away.

Get an Attorney

Once you've reached the point where an angel investor is seriously interested in your company and is beginning to negotiate the terms of the deal, you'll need an attorney. Whether you're raising $20,000 or $2 million, expert help at this stage is essential.

QUICK**TIP**

Hired Guns

You will have an ongoing relationship with your angel for many years, so you don't want to sour it during the negotiations. Attorneys can be the tough guys in negotiations. While it is professional and reasonable for you to speak up to make sure you are protected, let your attorney ask for the terms angels are more reluctant to grant.

Deal terms are complex—so complex that this book couldn't possibly cover them all. And terms change as investors devise new ways to protect their interests and rights. Moreover, many tax implications go along with issuing securities and establishing a valuation for a company.

You need an experienced securities attorney on your team. This means your *own* attorney, not just the angel's lawyer. That's not to say an attorney recommended by your angel can't represent you—experienced investors, especially in angel groups, will know knowledgeable lawyers. But make certain you consult with, and pay, an attorney yourself, to review any deal with an eye to protecting *you* and *your* interests, not just the interests of the company or the investor. A fair deal will protect everyone's rights.

1. What's on a term sheet

No two term sheets are exactly the same, although they share the same basic format. Your term sheet will be drafted to address the specific needs of your company and your investors' situation.

The term sheet is necessary because it will prevent issues from arising between the parties at a later stage that might prove to be deal killers. For instance, a new company might not realize that the investment it is receiving is "staged"— in other words, being delivered in stages linked to reaching certain milestones.

At a minimum, your term sheet will include:

- The agreed-upon company valuation and proposed capitalization table. (This will show the total amount of securities issued by your company.)

- The key financial and legal terms

- The rights of the parties

- All legal obligations of the parties

Here are some of the more common terms that you may come across in the term sheet or contract you draw up with your angel investor. Not all of these terms will be in your agreement, especially if it is a simple one. For a sample of a term sheet, see pages 161-168.

	WHAT IT MEANS	BE AWARE OF
	The person or company attempting to raise financing.	
Capitalization table (or "Cap table")	Table showing the total amount of securities issued by your company.	Typically, this includes the amount of investment obtained from each source and the type of securities involved—such as common or preferred shares, options, convertible notes, or warrants.
Type of security	Can be equity, debt, convertible preferred stock, or some combination.	Typically, angels want convertible preferred stock
Pre-money valuation	The valuation of your company prior to a round of investment.	Take your time over this. You can lose out if the valuation is either too low or too high.
Post-money valuation	The valuation of your company after a round of financing, calculated by adding the amount of funding invested in that round to the pre-money valuation.	
Warrant (or "stock purchase warrant" or "subscription warrant")	The right to purchase additional shares of common or preferred stock at a specified price over a defined period of time.	Know that warrants held by the investor or other third parties dilute your ownership further when exercised.
Convertible preferred stock	Stock that can be converted into common stock or another class of stock.	Investors may need to convert preferred stock into common stock prior to an initial public offering.
Preferred stock	Preferred stock comes with more rights, powers, and preferences than common stock.	Investors prefer this type of stock, and it is the type that angel investors usually want.

TERM	WHAT IT MEANS	BE AWARE OF
Convertible debt	A type of debt financing that allows a company's debt to be converted to equity, often at the option of the investor.	The conversion feature can be granted as a sweetener, since it provides the investor with the option of converting debt to equity if results are good.
Liquidation preference	Sets out the entitlements of the angel investor should your company fail.	If your company goes bankrupt, it may end up being worth very little, but your investor's liquidation preferences may result in their getting all the value, even if it is more than they invested.
Conversion and automatic conversion	Provisions for the right of preferred stockholders to convert their shares to common stock at the investor's discretion, or in the event of a public offering, with certain minimum provisions.	
Anti-dilution protection (or anti-dilution provisions)	Provisions to protect an angel investor against the dilutive effects of future sales of stock at lower prices. In other words, an agreement that entitles an angel investor to obtain additional equity in your company without additional cost should another investor purchase equity at a lower cost per share at a later stage.	Because anti-dilution provisions can result in protected investors receiving free shares of stock when a future funding is at a lower price, they can disproportionately reduce the percentage ownership of shareholders who are not protected. These "unprotected" shareholders usually include the company's founders and management.
Purchase agreement	This provision sets forth the fact that the binding document is yet to be drafted and will contain representations and warranties of the parties.	

TERM	WHAT IT MEANS	BE AWARE OF
Employee pool	Quantifies a set number of shares to be set aside as incentives for directors, officers, employees, and consultants.	This is a good thing to include, as it helps you attract key team members.
Protective provisions	These outline specific rights reserved for investors and address issues related to shares of stock or capital structure, board membership, the articles of incorporation, or a transfer in ownership.	This section will later make up the investor rights agreement.
Information rights	This provision sets out what is required of you in terms of providing information to your investor at regular intervals, such as monthly unaudited reports and audited annual reports.	Information rights can also include visitation and inspection rights for the investor at your place of business.
Registration rights	Contractual rights that entitle investors to force a company to register the investors' shares of company stock with the U.S. Securities and Exchange Commission (SEC) and state securities commissions.	

2. Negotiation

Once you are given a term sheet or a contract, go over the document with your attorney. If you have had your attorney prepare a contract for the investor, they'll review that document with their attorney.

The term sheet or contract may pass back and forth between you and your investor a number of times until it reflects an accurate understanding of the terms you've agreed upon and until you've worked out all the nitty-gritty details.

If you're negotiating with an angel group that invests as a group, you'll negotiate with either the manager or the lead angel. If you have multiple angels investing in your company at once, you'll negotiate first with the lead, or most important, angel, who will establish the terms that will affect all investors in the same round. Expect these negotiations to take 4 to 6 weeks, sometimes longer, especially if you are still negotiating matters such as the valuation of the company.

Be careful about agreeing to very restrictive provisions that are overly protective or overly generous to either your investors or you. Very restrictive provisions in the first round of financing can scare off investors in later rounds of financing who may be placed in a less-than-desirable situation because of these provisions.

Work with your attorney and make the provisions within your term sheet reasonable enough to attract follow-on investment. An experienced securities attorney knows what are considered reasonable or prohibitive terms. Pay close attention to liquidation preferences and anti-dilution protections.

Key Issues to Negotiate

- **Valuation.** Valuation is influenced by outside factors, such as valuations received by comparable companies, the price at which other companies in your industry have been acquired, and how much your company will eventually earn. Arm yourself by gathering as much of this information as possible before entering negotiations.

- **Equity division.** Ideally, after the first round of financing, you should still retain more than 50% ownership of your company. You can achieve this by lowering the amount of money you're seeking or by negotiating a higher valuation.

- **Employee (equity option) pool.** Ensure you have sufficient stock set aside so that you can attract and motivate key employees yet to be hired. If you do not set aside enough stock, you may find yourself having to dilute your own stock holdings at a future date to attract the candidates you want.

- **Anti-dilution provisions.** Investors care a great deal about anti-dilution. You will have to protect your early investors, but make certain the provisions are not so onerous that future investors will be scared off, making it hard to raise additional capital in subsequent rounds of financing. (See page 107 for more.)

- **Employment contract.** As part of the financing, you or your investors may want to negotiate an employment contract between you and the company. In the contract, specify your compensation, how long the agreement lasts, under what circumstances you can be terminated or replaced, and what will happen to your stock in that situation. Also negotiate what will happen to your stock if you leave the company voluntarily. Other terms to negotiate include any non-compete agreements (in states where they are legal) and ownership of intellectual property. Expect your investors to insist that the company's intellectual property must remain the sole property of the company.

- **Vesting schedule.** When stock is vested, it is transferred to the owner according to a certain schedule, not all at once. If possible, negotiate to have a certain percentage of your stock (typically 25%) vest immediately upon receiving financing, especially if you have already built the company substantially. Do not expect to get immediate stock vesting with a brand-new company. Other provisions in your vesting schedule might include restrictions on your ability to resell or transfer your stock to family members or third parties. (See page 124 for more.)

- **Liquidation preferences.** Investors routinely specify that, in the event the company is sold or closes, they have the option to receive their money back (in fact, often many times their original investment), rather than stock. In other words, if an angel invests $1 million and receives 33% of the stock, and the company is later sold for $2 million, the angel would receive $1 million, rather than merely one-third of the proceeds. If the investor negotiated a two-times multiple liquidation preference, the investor would get the entire $2 million, and the founders would receive nothing. You will want to keep liquidation preferences as low as possible, but investors will insist on these provisions.

- **Control.** Investors will specify what rights they have in terms of the operation of the company, such as a seat on the board of directors, receiving regular reports, and the terms under which they may remove you or other founders from management. Giving investors a board seat is normal, though angels often have to relinquish their board seats in later rounds if venture capitalists invest.

- **Milestones/Performance measures.** You and your investors may mutually agree upon specific milestone or performance measures before certain events can occur, such as having some of your stock vest or receiving subsequent payments of the angel's financial commitment. Try to avoid including such measures if possible. However, if they're included, make certain they are quantifiable, reasonable, and achievable. Such measures may include revenues, securing key customers, signing distribution or strategic partnership agreements, securing IP protections such as patents, and stages in product development such as prototype, beta testing, or first shipments.

Vesting

Even though a large percentage of the equity—or stock—in your company will be set aside for you and for other founders, you won't necessarily own all of your stock right from the start. Investors want to make sure you stay with the company. To ensure that you help build the company for a number of years, you'll have to earn your stock over time. In other words, you'll need to have your stock *vest*.

Vesting is a term that refers to the right to receive something at a future date—a right that cannot be taken away from you as long as certain conditions are met. One of the things you'll decide on during negotiations with your investors is how quickly you'll legally own the stock you're going to be entitled to. In other words, you'll be negotiating your *vesting schedule*. (You'll also negotiate a vesting schedule with any key employees you hire and to whom you offer stock.)

The primary reason that investors require you to vest your stock over a number of years is to make certain that you actually stay with the company and participate in building it over time. Imagine a scenario in which there was no vesting. An angel could fund your company and you could then take your share of the stock and leave. Any growth in the company would be entirely due to the work of others, but you would still own a huge share of the stock.

If you're starting a company with others, vesting is important from your personal point of view, as well. Let's say you're starting a business with two partners. After the first round of funding, you each end up with 20% of the company. Now, let's say that within a year, it's clear that one of your partners just can't perform at the level necessary. Is it fair that the person who leaves will end up owning the same amount of stock as you and your other partner, who will actually build the company? Vesting rewards those who stick with the company and makes certain that those who leave don't end up with disproportionate amounts of equity.

Vesting agreements usually cover a 3- to 5-year period. One of the most common vesting schedules is for 4 years, or 48 months. One-quarter of the founders' stock vests after 12 months, which means they will have no stock if they leave before the 12 months are up. The remainder of their stock will then continue to vest at the rate of 1/48th per month for the next 36 months.

One term you'll hear in relation to vesting is *cliff*, which refers to a steep change in vesting, rather than a gradual, month-by-month schedule. In the example above, there's a *cliff* after one year.

Another way that investors may want to structure your vesting is through a *performance-based* vesting schedule, rather than (or in conjunction with) calendar-based vesting. In other words, your stock vests upon completion of key milestones or events that are established at the time of funding. This is becoming increasingly popular, especially with sophisticated investors.

As part of the negotiations, you'll also be deciding on any conditions under which your stock will vest earlier than according to the agreed-upon schedule. This is called *accelerated vesting.*

Some vesting clauses to look for:

- "Immediate vesting of all stock if terminated other than for cause." In other words, if you are forced out of the company for a reason other than one specified in your employment contract, you would be entitled to all your stock.

- "Immediate vesting if and when the company is acquired by another company." If your company gets acquired, you'd want to have all your stock vest immediately so you wouldn't necessarily have to work for the new company. But your investors will *not* want this clause. They know that acquiring companies want to keep the principals involved and that you'll need an incentive to remain. Investors will often want a *two-trigger vesting clause* relating to acquisitions: one event that triggers accelerated vesting is the acquisition and the second event is if the acquiring company decides to let you go.

By the way, any unvested stock owned by you or anyone else on a vesting schedule goes back to the company if you (or that other person) leaves before the vesting period is finished.

It is *vital* to talk with a securities attorney and/or accountant to understand the tax implications of any stock or securities you receive and how your vesting schedule affects your taxes.

QUICK**TIP**

Stock Purchase Agreement

This is the formal name of the actual contract between you and your investors. It's also known as the "Investment Agreement" or the "Stock Purchase and Sale Agreement." The Stock Purchase Agreement sets forth the specific terms of the purchase and sale of the stock to the investors—such as the purchase price, closing date, conditions to close, and representations and warranties of the parties—and it identifies the other financing documents. If you and your angel agreed on a term sheet, the Stock Purchase Agreement would be based on the provisions spelled out there.

3. Sign the contract

After you and your investors have agreed in principle on the provisions contained in the term sheet (or the contract, if no term sheet is used), the due diligence process begins (see pages 131-136). Once due diligence is completed and the angel investors are satisfied, it's time to sign the actual contract.

If you have been negotiating from a contract, all you need to do now is sign the document. If you have been negotiating from a term sheet, the term sheet will be turned over to the lawyers, who will prepare a contract according to the provisions of the term sheet. There should be no surprises.

Prior to scheduling the actual signing of the contract and other legal documents, each party, along with their attorneys, should thoroughly review the contents of those documents. If you meet to sign documents (rather than signing them separately at your own attorneys' offices), you should be ready to pull out your pen and sign. No additional review or negotiations should be necessary at that point.

4. Get the money

After you get to the table to sign the final documents, expect to walk away with a check from your angel in hand or to receive it soon afterwards. In many cases, angels may transfer the funds directly from their bank account into your company's account. You should also find out whether they wish to do a bank transfer because in that case, you will have to give them the routing information for your business bank account.

Your angel will want to make the check out to your company or transfer the funds to the company's bank account, not to your personal account. So be sure to establish a business bank account earlier in the fundraising process.

You and your angel may have come to a deal that involves your receiving at this point only a portion of the money they've agreed to give you, with your company having to reach certain milestones in order to receive the rest of the funds. If that is the case, although your investor has legally agreed to their total financial commitment, the actual cash disbursements will be tied to those milestones. You won't receive all the funding up front. Discuss how and when the funds will be disbursed and have a written document detailing those disbursements.

Open a Business Account

When you are funded, your investors will want to deposit the money into your business bank account, not your personal account. Check to see whether your bank requires legal documents (such as incorporation papers) to open a business account, and get the process in motion as soon as you can.

Notes:

7

Accomplishments

In this Step you'll:

- ☐ 1. Discover what angels will investigate during due diligence
- ☐ 2. Find out who they will interview
- ☐ 3. Learn how angels assess your team

Time-Saving Tools

You'll complete this Step more quickly if you have any of the following handy:

- ☐ Contact information for your business and personal references
- ☐ An updated business plan
- ☐ All of your company's financial corporate records (financial statements, tax returns, articles of incorporation, shareholder information, and so on)
- ☐ List of all business contacts

Step 7:
Due Diligence

Before angel investors sign up to invest in your company and take on the risk that involves, they'll find out as much about you, your business, your product/service, and your industry as they can. This process, where the investor assesses the key aspects of your business in order to decide whether to invest, is known as "due diligence."

Individual angel investors often handle due diligence themselves. They'll occasionally contract with experts to verify market data and other assumptions, but generally they'll do their own investigation. They'll call your references to learn about your past accomplishments and determine your strengths and weaknesses as an entrepreneur and manager. Angels will often ask other businesspeople who are industry experts to review your business plans and verify your market analysis and assumptions.

QUICK**TIP**

Be Prepared

Help yourself and your investors by finding out up front what information they require. Ask for a list of information they'll need at the onset of the due diligence process. This will give you time to prepare data and to let friends and business contacts know that they may be approached by your potential investors.

If your potential angel investor belongs to an angel group that has a professional manager, that manager will oversee the due diligence process. The manager takes on specific duties, assigns others to members of the angel group, and contracts some of them out. The manager might assess your business plan and interview your management team and then hire a researcher to validate your market analysis. In angel groups that don't have professional management, a lead angel will head the due diligence process. If you have multiple angels, one will take the lead.

Angel investors call on a variety of experts to help them conduct due diligence. These include:

- Attorneys

- Accountants

- Market researchers

- Industry/technology/intellectual property experts

QUICK**TIP**

Accentuate the Positive

Have you had a start-up that didn't make it or declared bankruptcy in your past business life? These things are not necessarily deal killers. Be honest and tell your investors before they find out through due diligence. Explain the circumstances to your investors and be certain that you can explain to them exactly what you learned from the experience.

1. What angels investigate

During the due diligence process, all aspects of your business are investigated. Depending on the size of the investment, the stage of development your business is in, and whether you're working with an individual angel or an angel group, you'll be asked to provide certain business and technology documentation. Some angels require more and some less, depending on the amount of the investment, the angel's background, and whether the angel already knows you or has done business with you. Individual angels making smaller investments may come to your office themselves and review the necessary documents.

If you're working with a professional angel group, expect to spend weeks pulling together all the necessary paperwork. They will ask for everything from articles of incorporation to intellectual property rights to building leases.

You may be required to provide documents related to any or all of these areas:

Business

- Updated copy of your business plan

- Marketing materials

- Press releases and publicity

- Market research or assessment data

- Corporate records

- Articles or certificate of incorporation and by-laws or articles or certificate of organization of LLC and operating agreement

- Minutes from all board, committee, and shareholder meetings

- All stockholder and security holder information

- Business contracts (with suppliers, customers, distributors, consultants, and any other contract in excess of $1,000 or that has a significant impact on the business)

- List of all past, current, and pending business affiliations

Financial

- Financing or loans, letters of credit

- Relationships with financial institutions, investment bankers

- Liens, mortgages, encumbrances, guarantees, creditors

- Financial statements and tax returns for up to three years (if applicable)

- List of all accountants, bankers, and other financial advisors

Legal

- Any current or pending litigation regarding the company, its officers, or directors

- All documentation drafted by legal counsel

- Disclosure of any payment of finders' fees

- Any civil or criminal proceedings, convictions, court orders, or consent decrees

- Copies of any settlement agreements

- List of any legal counsel retained by the company

Property

- List and description of all owned or leased property

- All agreements (leases, deeds, construction contracts) pertaining to those properties

- Any appraisals or environmental reports

- An inventory of any personal property held by the business valued at $500 or more

Intellectual property

- List of all trademarks, trade names, service marks, copyrights, and patents

- List of all license and purchase agreements relating to intellectual property being used by the business

- Copy of any licenses, royalties, or other relationships

Management/employees

- Employment contracts

- Agreements with management, officers, or directors

- Copies of benefit plans

- Employment manual and organization chart

Insurance

- Copies of all policies, claims, and pending claims

Regulation compliance

- Disclosure of required permits and reporting, such as any related to OSHA (Occupational Safety and Health Administration) and EPA (Environmental Protection Agency)

- Disclosure of any communication involving regulatory agencies

Personal

- Any civil or criminal proceedings or convictions

- Disclosure of any bankruptcies

- Résumé, including education, work experience, and previous business start-ups

2. Who angels interview

Angel investors will also want to consult with people and businesses connected with you and your team. You'll be asked to give names of business references, and smart angels will dig a little deeper and find other people to talk to who have worked with you or your team. As they do this, they will be looking to verify information you've provided, as well as trying to learn more about your background, business style, and practices. Some angels do extensive background checks, while others are satisfied with talking to just a few people.

Some of the people angels may interview include:

- Employees
- Board members
- Competitors
- Business associates
- Former employers
- Customers and suppliers
- References
- Current accountant, attorney, and/or other service provider

3. How angels assess your team

First and foremost, angel investors will interview the founder and team members. To angel investors, the core team is as important as the business concept or technology innovation. After all, you and your co-workers are the ones who will make the company a success and ensure that the investment pays off. Among other things, angels assess:

- **Individual motivations.** Angels want to know why you are running or working for this business and what you want to achieve. They'll be looking to see if people are passionate about building a long-term, sustainable company or if they're just in it to try to make a quick buck.

- **Collective compatibility.** Team members' ability to work well together and complement each other in terms of skills and personalities is vital to a company's success and something angels are keenly interested in. Angels also try to find out if there are any major conflicts between staff members or divergent views on the company's direction.

- **Background accuracy.** Many angels check to confirm the accuracy of the information supplied on résumés regarding degrees and other honors. Outside services are often hired to conduct this background check.

- **Financial stability.** You and your team's personal financial situations may come under scrutiny. Be honest and ask your co-founders to be up front if they have had any financial issues and to disclose what they were and how they've been taken care of.

- **Quality of personal life.** Since they're investing a significant sum of money, angels care about the team members' personal lives. Upheavals such as divorce or serious illness that affect key executives' ability to focus on the business are of interest to an angel. Some angels are uncomfortable asking personal questions directly, so they'll ask others who know you about your personal life.

- **Commitment to the business.** Assuming the angel believes the founding team is composed of the right people to make the business a success, they have a vested interest in having them stay for the long haul. Expect direct questions about how strongly you and your team believe in the business and how much time, effort, and personal money you're willing to invest in it.

Accomplishments

In this Step you'll:

☐ 1. Find out how often you'll meet with your investor(s)

☐ 2. Discover how long your relationship with an angel will last

☐ 3. Explore follow-on funding and exit strategies

Time-Saving Tools

You'll complete this Step more quickly if you have the following handy:

☐ A copy of your term sheet or contract

Step 8:
After the Deal

Once you have successfully secured angel funding, it's time to focus on developing and growing your business. Depending on what stage your company is in, that could mean launching new products and services, recruiting employees, focusing on the day-to-day operations, or working on getting your first customers.

Remember your angel investors are on board with you now too—often quite literally as a member of your board of directors. Even when they're not on the board, most angels want to participate in your business at some level. For instance, they'll help entrepreneurs locate high-quality executives by tapping into their networks to find suitable candidates. At a minimum, they'll require you to keep them up to date about your financial situation. A good investor is also on call for you. Don't hesitate to reach out to your angel for advice and information.

All angels have certain expectations in terms of how you run the business and report to them. They expect you to:

- Manage the day-to-day operations and performance of the business

- Manage progress toward and reach goals and established milestones

- Deliver reporting requirements in a timely manner

- Provide regular financial updates, usually monthly or quarterly

- Give your commitment and passion to the business. This may mean that the business comes before friends and family at times.

- Report any unexpected challenges or possible missed milestones ahead of time (Remember: Your angel may be able to help you solve such problems.)

1. How often should you meet with your angels?

Angels vary as to how much they want to meet with the companies they invest in. Some individual investors are entirely hands off, but that's the exception, rather than the rule. Most angels expect at least quarterly meetings, where they will hear a report on financials and business progress.

How often you meet with your investors depends on:

- What you have agreed to in the written documentation of your deal

- What type of angel you have (see opposite page)

The best indicator of how you'll interact with your angel is how you got along in the courtship phase. During that time you will have come to know your angel over the course of numerous meetings. A good relationship at that point usually translates into a good relationship once the contract is signed. Once you and your angel have come to this agreement, you'll determine a regular meeting schedule. Other ongoing communication will be conducted over the phone, via email, or at occasional meetings, lunches, or dinners.

An angel investors' involvement in your business is also tied to how well the business is performing. If the business is underperforming or failing to meet established milestones, most angels will become more engaged or seek out professional management for your company. If their investment is threatened, it is possible that your role as leader of the company could change. In rare instances, and if the terms of your contract provide for it, angel investors can oversee the removal of the company's founder.

The Different Types
of Angel Investors

Angels come in all sorts of flavors. Depending on the terms you have agreed upon, you may have one of the following angel investor types:

- **The coach.** These angels are your trusted advisors. They're always available and willing to share advice and wisdom. They'll even roll up their sleeves and pitch in when the situation demands it. This is the best kind of investor.

- **In the starting line-up.** Some angels take an active role in the day-to-day operation of the business. Their role could be limited to a few hours a week or, if the company needs it, a commitment equal to the entrepreneur's.

- **On the bench.** These angels are not regularly involved in the running of your business, but they are available to a limited extent should the need arise.

- **Spectator.** Angels like this don't want to be actively involved in your company, and their expectations are limited to regular financial reporting.

- **The boss.** This is an angel who effectively takes over (known as a "George Steinbrenner type," after the principal owner of the New York Yankees, who has a reputation for being extremely hands on). This type of relationship works well in situations where the founder is the technical or creative genius and does not want, or does not have the skills, to be a CEO.

Make the Most of Your Angel

If you've chosen your angels well, they will provide more than just money to help the growth of your business. So engage your angel. They may have taken an interest in your business because they have product expertise or contacts in the industry. They may bring a skill set that is underrepresented in the business. Frequently, angels serve in a financial advisory or leadership role as part of the management team.

This opportunity to engage with your funders increases substantially if your funding comes through an angel network. The lead angel acts as the point person, disseminating information to the rest of the network. Within that network there is a breadth of expertise, covering many, if not all, aspects of your specific business. Look at this as a jackpot of talent for your company.

2. How long will this relationship last?

Your angel investor has a legal and financial relationship with the company as long as their money is still in the company. In other words, the relationship between your company and the angel investor lasts until there is some type of liquidity event, a point at which they can get their money out.

But the angel's active relationship with you and your company depends on the individual angel, the nature of their involvement with your business, and whether they participate in subsequent rounds of financing.

Sometimes a relationship with an angel evolves from business partner to advisor and trusted friend, and the relationship lasts as long as the entrepreneur is running the company. In contrast, some professional angel investors have limited amounts of time to allocate to the companies in which they invest. These types of angels will want to move on to the next start-up once the current company is meeting its goals and running smoothly.

If your company requires another round of funding and new investors come in with substantially more money (for example, with Series B funding), the influence of your Series A angel will be reduced. The new funders will set most of the terms and conditions for the strategic growth of your business. Depending on the size of the round, this new group might assume board positions or even board control. At this point, the Round A angels will sometimes relinquish their board seats or at a minimum, assume a minority position on the board. This does not apply, however, if your first-round angel is the lead in the second round of funding.

Will My Angel Investors Lead Me to a VC?

As your business grows, you may need more money—possibly a lot more money than can be provided by an angel investor. You may want to turn to a venture capitalist (VC). Will your angel help lead you to a VC?

First, you will need to determine whether your business will meet the minimum threshold for venture-capital investment as it grows. Generally, VCs invest a minimum of $5 million, but some boutique VC firms will invest as little as $2 million to $3 million.

Analyze your long-term capital financing needs. If those projections reach the minimum venture-capital threshold, it's a good idea to ask about your angel's contacts and relationships in the venture-capital community before selecting your next investor. Pre-established relationships with VCs, or a history of co-investments, make it much easier and less time consuming to raise subsequent funds. In some cases, VC connections end up being one of the most important contributions an angel investor makes to a company.

Consider the following when deciding whether you need venture capital:

- What are the capital requirements over the life of your business?

- Does the angel investor have adequate capital to fund all the needs of the business?

- What relationship does the angel investor have with the venture-capital community?

Relationships between angel investors and venture capitalists soured somewhat after the dot-com era, partly because some angel investors suffered significant dilution at the hands of venture capitalists. Those issues contributed to the rise of angel investor groups. By collectively investing capital, angel groups avoided venture capital participation. Today, tensions have cooled off, and angel investors and venture capitalists each recognize the significant contributions that the other makes to the funding cycle of a business.

3. Follow-on funding

As your company develops, you may need a number of subsequent funding rounds, including venture capital, to reach the goals you and your investors set for the business. Your initial angel investors may participate in these later rounds, and this typically makes the funding rounds easier and faster. On the other hand, each round could see a new cast of characters, which means you will start the financing process all over again from scratch.

Be sure your business needs the money before you decide on subsequent rounds. Consider other types of financing that might be available to you, such as bank loans. Remember: With each round of funding, all previous shareholders, including you, will face additional dilution.

Subsequent rounds of funding should be used to build a bigger business. Your investors' primary goal is to be able to exit the business and "harvest" the return on their investment. So always keep your exit strategy in mind when considering how additional funding rounds will help build the business until it reaches your projected exit point.

The chart opposite outlines exit strategy options to consider as your company matures.

Exit Plan Options

OPTION	DESCRIPTION	BENEFITS	DRAWBACKS
Go public	Sell stock in the company on a public stock exchange	The stock easily converts to cash; liquidity	Must be a large company; approx. $25 to $50 million; highly regulated
Acquisition	Another company buys yours	Investors receive cash and/or stock	Must be a good fit for the existing company; company must have clear value
Sale	Individuals buy the company	Investors get cash	Must find a willing buyer; company must have clear value
Merger	Join with an existing company	Investors may receive stock in the new company or some cash	Usually little or no cash; stock may not be easily traded
Buy-Out	One or more current shareholders buy out the interest of another	Sellers get cash	Buyer must have sufficient cash; often contentious negotiations
Franchise	Replicate concept by licensing rights to others	Receive cash; franchisees finance expansion	Concept must be appropriate; legally complicated

Troubleshooting

Why Won't Angels Fund My Business?

If you are meeting many angel investors but none have offered to invest in your company, start by figuring out at what stage in the process you're losing them. Are they turning you down when they see your business plan? Or do they say "no" later in the process? Noting when they turn you down may provide some insight into where adjustments need to be made. Consider the following:

- **Your business concept is flawed.** If you're hearing the same objections over and over again, take a look at your business concept. Conduct new research, re-evaluate your assumptions, and adjust your plan accordingly.

- **Someone else should do the presentation.** Ask yourself whether you are the right person to do the presentation. It's easy to be passionate about your product, but what investors really want to hear about are the business and financial opportunities. Try having a finance or marketing executive present the material.

- **Your ego is getting in the way.** Angels want someone with a healthy ego, but they also want an executive who will listen and take direction when needed.

Be honest with yourself: Do you have a tendency to come off as a know-it-all? Are you an active listener during the funding meetings? Ask your friends and co-workers for feedback.

- **You're talking to the wrong people.** Do the people you are meeting with fit the profile of someone who would actually fund your business? Review whether you fit *their* criteria, whether their skills complement your business, and whether they have made similar investments.

- **You don't have a fundable deal.** There may not be an adequate market for your product or service. Your financial projections may not be realistic or provide a desirable return on investment. Have an outside expert evaluate your plan and provide recommendations.

- **Your team is incomplete.** Look at your management team and see if there are any key members missing. If your company's success is based primarily on consumer branding and you don't have an ace marketing person in place, this would concern most angels. It's not unusual for start-up companies to bring on new key executives in order to attract funding.

Something Went Wrong with My Presentation ... Now What?

Many different disasters can occur in the middle of a presentation—anything from a technology issue to a failed product demonstration. Do your best to avoid such situations by:

- Arriving early and doing a dry run of the presentation

- Knowing who is going to be in the audience

- Expecting the unexpected. Stay calm and remain positive and professional in your exchanges, no matter what happens.

- Clarifying beforehand what equipment is available and what equipment you should take with you

- Taking multiple presentation formats, such as a flash drive and CD, to the meeting. Always email the presentation to yourself so it can be remotely accessed. And in case the technology still lets you down, take hard copies of your presentation to hand out.

- Practicing ... over and over and over ...

- Reading The Planning Shop's *Winning Presentation In A Day*, available at bookstores or online at *www.planningshop.com.*

Every entrepreneur faces situations where things do not go perfectly. If something does occur that you can't fix on the spot, apologize when appropriate, but stay focused and continue with your presentation. Consider such challenges opportunities to prove your resilience under unexpected pressure.

What Happens If I Don't Meet My Milestones?

Milestones and the consequences of failing to reach them will be spelled out in the terms of your deal. The results of failing to meet agreed-upon milestones can include:

- The investor understands what's going on and stands by with full faith and financial commitment to your business.

- If additional funding is tied to reaching specific milestones, and those milestones are not reached, investors can withhold part or all of the additional funding.

- The investor provides additional funding tied to reaching the milestone but takes additional ownership in the business, further diluting your ownership interest.

- You and/or other members of the management team are replaced.

Why Has My Relationship with My Angel Investors Gone Sour?

If your relationship with your investors has deteriorated, it may be because you haven't been keeping them informed and involved in the company—particularly if the business is underperforming. Under-performance generally stems from one or more of these four main issues:

- **Money.** Your business burns through the funding faster than anticipated and is unable to raise subsequent rounds of funding.

- **Product.** The product fails to perform as expected.

- **Customer acceptance.** Customers are not buying the product as projected or the market size was overestimated.

- **Team.** Management has made missteps or underperformed by missing milestones or other established goals.

Investors are hesitant to put additional money into a company when the problem is product based or customer based. If your business has gone off course and your investor controls the board of directors or owns a controlling interest in the company, you and/or members of your team could be replaced.

Keeping your investors informed before major trouble occurs can ward off catastrophes. They want the business to succeed and will do what they can to help meet challenges.

10 Sure-Fire Ways to Fail with Angel Investors

1. Not having a high-quality business plan.

2. Focusing on the product/service, rather than the business model.

3. Underestimating angel investors (saying, for instance: "This is very complex, so you probably won't understand … ")

4. Approaching the wrong angels (they invest more/less than you need; they don't invest in your industry).

5. Attracting dumb, rather than smart, money. Can the angel bring more to the table than just money?

6. Failing to do due diligence on your angel and having a bad relationship—you need to get along.

7. Having too many small investors.

8. Having too much ego. Learn to listen and evaluate.

9. Hiding information from your angels—they will find out.

10. Not starting with the end (exit) in mind. Investors invest only when you have a plan to sell the company to someone else or go public.

The Experts Talk

Wouldn't it be wonderful if you could enter the minds of the people who will fund your business—if you could learn what kinds of companies they look for, how they evaluate your business plan, and how they expect to be involved with the company?

Now you can. On the pages that follow, you'll find interviews with four angels. They'll tell you in their own words:

- What makes a company an attractive investment opportunity

- How much money they will invest

- What they look for in a management team

- What they consider to be red flags and critical mistakes in business plans and proposals

Before you seek an angel investor, learn from the experts interviewed here. Use their real-life experience to help you prepare to look for funding. Their insights into everything from how they judge financial projections to how they perform due diligence will help you find the right angel and make the right pitch.

Mark Leiter

Mark Leiter, a nationally known expert in strategic marketing and services innovation, is Chairman of Leiter & Company and a member of the New York Angels, one of America's largest angel groups, with 75 members. New York Angels provides seed and early-stage capital in the range of $250K–$750K to technology, new media, and professional services companies in the Northeast. Mark has co-founded and/or invested in half a dozen companies in the past seven years.

What kinds of companies do you invest in?

I invest in what I know: professional and business services such as management consultants, marketing and advertising, executive recruiting, and high-end business-to-business companies. I'm interested in start-ups, rather than later-stage companies. Not everyone has the stomach for start-ups. I will consider a guy with just a business plan because I want a larger stake and the chance to influence the business.

What is the range of money you invest?

Between $25,000 and $100,000.

What percentage ownership do you have in the companies you invest in?

Anywhere between 0.5% and 30%, with the higher end of the range representing situations when I'm helping start the company in a very "hands-on" manner.

Why do you invest in start-ups?

Unlike buying stocks or bonds, investing in start-ups is like signing up for an adventure. In some ways you are getting married to that company, and what happens after the investment is as important to me as what happened before because I'm interested in helping companies.

What makes a company attractive to you as an investment opportunity?

I bet on people more than on concepts. I mostly invest in people I have known professionally for many years. I have a sense of who they are and what they are doing. By the time I am ready to write the check, I'm pretty sure about what I'm getting into.

What sort of deal flow do you see?

Being part of an angel group is great for deal flow. The New York Angels screen hundreds of proposals each year, and all its members are invited to see three or four presentations every month.

What rate of return do you expect for your investments?

A positive one! Angel investing can easily turn into a rich man's hobby because you can lose a lot of money. The best way to approach it is to diversify and hope that for the many companies that provide you with no return, you'll get lucky and one will give you a 500% return! But if you're looking for guaranteed 20%–30% return, angel investing is the wrong game for you.

What do you feel is the most critical mistake entrepreneurs make in their business plans?

Entrepreneurs are too optimistic in their projections. But it's a Catch 22 because investors expect them to be overly optimistic and they discount for it, so entrepreneurs can't afford to be too realistic/pessimistic. It's a psychological game. Entrepreneurs lack the resources necessary to do good analysis, so the investor is flying without a lot of information. In the end you are betting on the team and its judgment.

What are the deal breakers for you? What would make you reject a proposal immediately?

There are two. First, I won't invest in anything outside my area of expertise, however glamorous or enticing a proposal may appear. I take the Warren Buffett approach that you stick to what you know. Second, I have zero tolerance for first start-ups—such as the person coming out of a big, resource-rich firm, who is launching a business for the first time. These people make lots of mistakes. Let someone else take that risk. Entrepreneurs on their second or third try have the battle scars, and they are the ones who are more likely to be successful.

What is the most important factor when valuing a company for investment? Do you have a process you favor for valuation? What mistakes do entrepreneurs make when valuing their companies?

Valuation is a dark science—and a dark art. You can take the scientific approach and crunch all the numbers, look at the competition and so on, and rationalize a base valuation. But so much is based on a conviction of where the company is going to be in two years' time. And that is partly subjective. If an entrepreneur exudes confidence and the investor is excited, the valuation goes up. If the founder hits obstacles, they lose a key member of the team for instance, that can be a blow. Investors know that the emotions of the entrepreneur go up and down, and they play on that. (They only talk about it among themselves, though!)

What due diligence do you conduct on a company you are going to invest in?

The most important due diligence I do is spending time talking to the team about where they are going and what their plan is. I look to make sure there is a balance between the people and the technology and that the management team is pointed in the right direction. The technical due diligence, talking to customers, taking up references—that's important, too, of course.

What sort of involvement do you expect in the companies you finance?

I hope that my contribution will go far beyond providing money. A healthy deal is one where the investor is involved. I expect and hope that companies will come back to me at some point in the journey and ask for introductions to clients—or more money.

Laura Roden

Laura Roden is the Managing Director of The Angels' Forum, an angel investor group with 25 members based in Palo Alto, California. Previously, she was the Chief Executive Officer of SVASE, the Silicon Valley Association of Start-Up Entrepreneurs, a non-profit dedicated to helping early-stage entrepreneurs build successful companies in the technology sectors.

What kinds of companies do you invest in?

We invest in four areas: information technology (hardware, software, e-commerce, and Web 2.0), medical devices, consumer and retail, and clean-tech and energy-related businesses.

What is the range of money you invest?

For a typical Series A round, Angels' Forum's share would be anywhere between $250,000 and $750,000. We often stay with the companies through Series B and Series C rounds and can end up investing a total of $3 million in one company.

What makes a company attractive to you as an investment opportunity?

It needs to meet our five investment criteria. The CEO and CFO need to be based in the San Francisco Bay area. It needs to be in one of our four industry categories (see above). It must have a CEO—we see lots of companies headed up by a founder or a scientist, but we won't invest unless they have a CEO in place. It must be able to demonstrate proof of concept, so not still be at the concept stage. We want to see a working prototype or beta application. And, finally, we only invest in companies we believe won't need more than $25 million before they break even.

What sort of deal flow do you see?

Angels' Forum sees 15 to 20 potential deals a week—about a thousand a year.

Where do your potential investments come from? How do they find you?

Most of the companies we see come to us through word of mouth—especially through lawyers, bankers, and accountants whom we work with through the network. Some approach us after having seen us speaking at events. And a few apply to us online through our website.

Are you approached by matchmaking services offering companies to invest in? If so, have you found them to be effective?

We don't deal with business brokers. We do work with a few consultants who we know well and who spend time working with the management of start-ups and then help them get funding.

What do you look for in a business plan?

We ask companies to produce a one-page "deal snapshot," and that is the first thing we review, before even looking at the business plan.

What are the deal breakers for you? What would make you reject a proposal immediately?

A company that doesn't meet our investment criteria (see above) is disqualified immediately.

What due diligence do you conduct on a company you are going to invest in?

We do background checks for criminal records and the like, and our members who are very knowledgeable about the field the company is operating in conduct due diligence by getting to know the management team and talking informally with people who know them.

What sort of involvement do you expect in the companies you finance?

We usually take a seat on the board—although we expect to lose that to a larger investor later on down the line. One angel member will also be a relationship manager with the company. They may speak to the CEO once a week, and once a quarter we spend an entire day reviewing the status of all existing portfolio companies, for which each entrepreneur prepares a financial and strategic "self-review."

If you had one piece of advice for entrepreneurs looking for angel investment, what would it be?

I would say put yourself in the investor's shoes. So often, when we ask the entrepreneurs how we are going to get our money out at the end of the deal, they just look at us blankly. And how we are going to get our money out is ultimately the thing investors care most about! About 50% of the companies we see don't tailor the way they speak to us. They are just thinking about their business idea and how good it is and not considering what the investor is interested in.

Jeff Stinson

Jeff Stinson is Executive Director of the Fund for Arkansas' Future, an angel investor fund that provides capital to early-stage Arkansas-based companies. The Fund, which aims to drive economic development in Arkansas through the creation of high-growth companies based in the state, has 57 members and a capital commitment of $6.6 million. Since its launch in early 2005, it has invested in three companies and is conducting due diligence on several more.

What kinds of companies do you invest in?

To date we have invested in very different types of companies, including a for-profit incubator, a bio-fuels business, and a company with a proprietary skincare product. The common factor is that they are all Arkansas-based and they meet our second criterion: they have the chance to grow rapidly.

What is the range of money you invest?

We have a $6.6 million fund, and we average about $250,000 per company.

What are your investment criteria?

The companies must be based in Arkansas and have the ability to grow quickly.

Where do your potential investments come from? How do they find you?

Many companies hear about us through word of mouth, some apply directly through our website, and others meet us at our speaking engagements around the state. Our investments also make the news because we are one of the few sources of early-stage capital in Arkansas.

What is the average time between when you receive a business plan and when you close on an investment?

90 days.

What rate of return do you expect for your investments?

As high as possible, because the risk with angel investing is so inordinately high. In a portfolio of companies, half will probably go out of business, which means we lose all of our investment; a few will provide modest returns; and one or two will be the "home runs" that provide the bulk of the returns.

What makes a company attractive to you as an investment opportunity?

We invest in people. Because we fund mostly pure start-ups, we are taking a high risk. And the most important way to reduce the risk is to be as confident as you can be in the abilities of the people behind the company—the management team.

What are the red flags for you when assessing an investment proposal?

It's often an issue of scale. Too many business models don't have the rate of growth we are looking for. Businesses such as a hair salon, a deli, or a bowling alley may provide enough revenue for the founder's lifestyle, but they won't make the $20 million in annual revenues in five years that we seek.

What mistakes do entrepreneurs make when presenting their companies to you?

They haven't thought completely through and/or aren't candid with us regarding such issues as market size, competition, customer needs, their sustainable competitive advantage, how the market will change over time, their own management abilities, and so on. I would say only 20% of the companies are well prepared when they present to us.

What due diligence do you conduct on a company you are going to invest in?

We do more than a rich uncle and less than a venture-capital firm would do. Our investment committee of seven people spends 30 to 45 days learning as much as it can about a prospect—the team, validating the market and the customers, looking at patents and the competition. We write up a due diligence report, which is circulated before we take a final vote on whether to invest.

What sort of involvement do you expect in the companies you finance?

As well as capital, we provide mentoring, monitoring, and strategic help. What you provide on top of the funds affects the investment ultimately. We always assign one of our members to the company's board of directors.

Larry Fenster

Larry Fenster is based in Denver, Colorado, and has been an independent angel investor for 10 years, during which time he has invested sums ranging from $25,000 to $200,000 in 20 companies. Larry was formerly President of Natkin Energy Management, a Colorado-based energy performance service company, which was later sold to ServiceMaster Inc. He was Executive Vice President of ServiceMaster and responsible for several business units. He founded Global Facility Solutions, a facility management outsourcing company.

What kinds of companies do you invest in?

I mainly invest in companies that are connected to my background in energy services and the medical field. The companies are usually in the start-up stage, although some need growth capital. I do make the odd tangential deal—I fly airplanes, so I invested in an aviation simulation software company. I often co-invest with other angels.

What makes a company attractive to you as an investment opportunity?

I have a screening process that determines whether I want to spend time with a company and potentially invest. It's based on three things: the management team, the idea, and the deal structure. The management team accounts for a majority of the decision. I have learned through experience that having a strong leader and a strong team is essential to building a successful business.

What sort of deal flow do you see?

I see several hundred deals a year, of which I invest in one or two. Many of the deals fall outside my areas of expertise, so I don't invest in them.

Where do your potential investments come from? How do they find you?

My deal flow comes through my personal network and also several organizations I belong to. Most of the deals are the result of a personal referral from a trusted source. Some come to me through local incubators, and some via attorneys or accountants who provide a referral.

What rate of return do you expect for your investments?

I typically expect to see an IRR (Internal Rate of Return) of 40% to 50% for a start-up company with a typical risk profile. This equates to a return of ten dollars for each dollar of investment for a five-year term.

What do you look for in the founders/management team?

There are two types of management teams: serial experienced entrepreneurs and entrepreneurs who are working on their first start-up. I look for experienced entrepreneurs who have demonstrated their ability to succeed in their prior careers. I especially like it if an entrepreneur has had a successful prior venture that made money for the investors. I also like to see a diverse management team with individuals who have most of the skill sets required to start and grow the business.

What are the red flags for you when assessing an investment proposal?

Many times an entrepreneur will have an interesting idea, but they haven't thought through the sales, marketing, finance, and operational issues necessary to start and grow the business. Some entrepreneurs underestimate the time, money, and resources necessary to support a start-up business. Entrepreneurs believe that since they have a "great idea," it will be easy to sell it to customers. This is often a result of not knowing the competition or having a focused business development strategy.

What are the deal breakers for you?

An inadequate management team is clearly a deal breaker. So is a poorly thought-out and presented business plan. Excessive valuations and unrealistic projections are deal breakers. And I always expect strong references.

What mistakes do entrepreneurs make when valuing their companies?

Inexperienced entrepreneurs create unrealistic financial projections and underestimate the amount of time and money required to start and grow their venture. They base a valuation on these unrealistic projections and create an unrealistic valuation. Entrepreneurs should do their homework on the methods for valuing early-stage ventures, including finding out what comparable companies in a similar stage and market have historically

received. An excessive valuation is a disincentive for angels.

What due diligence do you conduct on a company you are going to invest in?

I always invest in companies that are within an hour's drive from my house. I will often take on a role as an advisor/mentor with an early-stage company I'm interested in for several months. This allows me to help the entrepreneur and also to fully get to know them, the management team, and the business. This is the very best due diligence you can do for a start-up company.

What sort of involvement do you expect in the companies you finance?

I am an active investor. I invest time and money, and I'm willing to work with an entrepreneur before I invest. After I invest I'm in regular contact with the entrepreneur by phone and email. I may also sit in on a start-up's weekly management committee meeting and help the entrepreneur at special meetings with key customers and potential investors. I generally don't want to be on a board of directors because of liability issues. Most early-stage companies can't afford directors' liability insurance. A good solution is to use an advisory board that doesn't expose the directors to liability.

Sample
Term Sheet

SUMMARY OF TERMS FOR PROPOSED PRIVATE PLACEMENT
OF SERIES A PREFERRED STOCK AND WARRANTS OF
LIME TREE, INC.
NOVEMBER 28, 2007

Issuer: Lime Tree, Inc., a Delaware corporation (the "Company")

Investor(s):   Eagle Ventures

Amount of Financing: $200,000

Price: $0.40 per share for the Series A Preferred Stock and $0.01 for the associated common warrants. ("Original Purchase Price"). For each share of Series A Preferred stock purchased, an investor will have the right to purchase a warrant exercisable for one share of common stock. The exercise price of the warrant shall be $0.01 per common share and the term of the warrant shall be 5 years. The Original Purchase Price represents a fully-diluted pre-money valuation of approximately $800,000 and a fully-diluted post money valuation of approximately $1 million.

Type of Security: Series A Convertible Preferred Stock (the "Series A Preferred"), initially convertible on a 1:1 basis into shares of the Company's Common Stock (the "Common Stock") and associated warrants for common stock.

TERMS OF SERIES A PREFERRED STOCK

Dividends:

The holders of the Series A Preferred shall be entitled to receive non-cumulative dividends in preference to any dividend on the Common Stock at the rate of 8% of the Original Purchase Price per annum, when and as declared by the Board of Directors. The holders of Series A Preferred also shall be entitled to participate pro rata in any dividends paid on the Common Stock on an as-if-converted basis.

Liquidation Preference:

In the event of any liquidation or winding up of the Company, the holders of the Series A Preferred shall be entitled to receive a per share amount equal to three times the Original Purchase Price plus any declared but unpaid dividends (the "Liquidation Preference").

After the payment of the Liquidation Preference to the holders of the Series A Preferred, the remaining assets shall be distributed ratably to the holders of the Common Stock and the Series A Preferred.

Conversion:

The holders of the Series A Preferred shall have the right to convert the Series A Preferred, at any time, into shares of Common Stock. The initial conversion rate shall be 1:1, subject to adjustment as provided below.

Automatic Conversion:

The Series A Preferred shall be automatically converted into Common Stock, at the then applicable conversion price, (i) in the event that the holders of at least a majority of the outstanding Series A Preferred consent to such conversion or (ii) upon the closing of a firmly underwritten public offering of shares of Common Stock of the Company at a per share price not less than four times the Original Purchase Price (as adjusted for stock splits, dividends and the like) per share and for a total offering of not less than $25 million (before deduction of underwriters' commissions and expenses) (a "Qualified IPO").

Anti-dilution:

The conversion price of the Series A Preferred will be subject to a full ratchet adjustment to eliminate dilution in the event that the Company issues additional equity securities (other than shares reserved as employee shares described under "Employee Pool" below) at a purchase price less than the applicable conversion price. The conversion price will also be subject to proportional adjustment for stock splits, stock dividends, recapitalizations and the like.

Redemption at Option of Investors:	At the election of the holders of at least a majority of the Series A Preferred, the Company shall redeem the outstanding Series A Preferred in three annual installments beginning on the fifth anniversary of the Closing. Such redemptions shall be at a purchase price equal to the Original Purchase Price plus declared and unpaid dividends.
Voting Rights:	The Series A Preferred will vote together with the Common Stock and not as a separate class except as specifically provided herein or as otherwise required by law. Each share of Series A Preferred shall have a number of votes equal to the number of shares of Common Stock then issuable upon conversion of such share of Series A Preferred.
Board of Directors:	The size of the Company's Board of Directors shall be set at five. The Board shall initially be composed of two members elected by the common stockholders, one of whom shall be the company's CEO, and three people nominated by Eagle Ventures.
Protective Provisions:	For so long as any shares of Series A Preferred remain outstanding, consent of the holders of at least a majority of the Series A Preferred shall be required for any action that (i) alters or changes the rights, preferences or privileges of the Series A Preferred, (ii) increases or decreases the authorized number of shares of Common or Preferred Stock, (iii) creates (by reclassification or otherwise) any new class or series of shares having rights, preferences or privileges senior to or on a parity with the Series A Preferred, (iv) results in the redemption or repurchase of any shares of Common Stock (other than redemptions at cost pursuant to equity incentive agreements with service providers giving the Company the right to repurchase shares upon the termination of services), (v) results in any merger, other corporate reorganization, sale of control, or any transaction in which all or substantially all of the assets of the Company are sold, (vi) amends or waives any provision of the Company's Articles of Incorporation or Bylaws relative to the Series A Preferred, (vii) increases or decreases the authorized size of the Company's Board of Directors, (viii) results in the payment or declaration of any dividend on any shares of Common or Preferred Stock, or (ix) results in the issuance of debt in excess of $100,000.

Information Rights:

So long as an Investor continues to hold shares of Series A Preferred or Common Stock issued upon conversion of the Series A Preferred, the Company shall deliver to the Investors audited annual and unaudited quarterly and monthly financial statements (compared against the Company's operating plan). The Company shall also deliver to the Investors within 30 days prior to the beginning of each fiscal year a copy of the Company's annual operating plan. Each Investor shall also be entitled to standard inspection and visitation rights. These provisions shall terminate upon a Qualified IPO.

Registration Rights:

Demand Rights: If Investors holding more than 50% of the outstanding shares of Series A Preferred, including Common Stock issued on conversion of Series A Preferred ("Registrable Securities"), or a lesser percentage if the anticipated aggregate offering price to the public is not less than $5,000,000, request that the Company file a Registration Statement, the Company will use its best efforts to cause such shares to be registered; provided, however, that the Company shall not be obligated to effect any such registration prior to the third anniversary of the Closing. The Company shall have the right to delay such registration under certain circumstances for one period not in excess of ninety (90) days in any twelve (12) month period.

The Company shall not be obligated to effect more than three (3) registrations under these demand right provisions, and shall not be obligated to effect a registration (i) during the one hundred eighty (180) day period commencing with the date of the Company's initial public offering, or (ii) if it delivers notice to the holders of the Registerable Securities within thirty (30) days of any registration request of its intent to file a registration statement for such initial public offering within ninety (90) days.

Company Registration: The Investors shall be entitled to "piggy-back" registration rights on all registrations of the Company or on any demand registrations of any other investor subject to the right, however, of the Company and its underwriters to reduce the number of shares proposed to be registered pro rata in view of market conditions. If the Investors are so limited, however, no party shall sell shares in such registration other than the Company or the Investor, if any, invoking the demand registration. Unless the registration is with respect to the Company's initial public offering, in no event shall the shares to be sold by the Investors be reduced below 30% of the total amount of securities included in the registration. No stockholder of the Company shall be granted piggyback registration rights which would reduce the number of shares includable by the holders of the Registerable Securities in such registration without the consent of the holders of at least two-thirds of the Registerable Securities.

S-3 Rights: Investors shall be entitled to unlimited demand registrations on Form S-3 (if available to the Company) so long as such registered offerings are not less than $1,000,000.

Expenses: The Company shall bear registration expenses (exclusive of underwriting discounts and commissions) of all such demand, "piggy-back", and S-3 registrations (including the expense of one special counsel of the selling stockholders not to exceed $25,000).

Transfer of Rights: The registration rights may be transferred to (i) any partner or retired partner of any holder which is a partnership, (ii) any member or former member of any holder which is a limited liability company, (iii) any family member or trust for the benefit of any individual holder, or (iv) any transferee who is or that satisfies the criteria to be a Major Investor (as defined below); provided the Company is given written notice thereof.

Lock-Up Provision: Each Investor agrees that it will not sell its shares for a specified period (but not to exceed 180 days) following the effective date of the Company's initial public offering; provided that all officers, directors, and other 1% stockholders are similarly bound.

Other Provisions: Other provisions shall be contained in the Investor Rights Agreement with respect to registration rights as are reasonable, including cross-indemnification, the period of time in which the Registration Statement shall be kept effective, and underwriting arrangements.

Right of First Refusal: Investors who purchase at least seventy thousand (70,000) shares of Series A Preferred (a "Major Investor") shall have the right in the event the Company proposes to offer equity securities to any person (other than the shares reserved as employee shares described under "Employee Pool" below or securities issued pursuant to acquisitions and strategic transactions) to purchase their pro rata portion of such shares. Any securities not subscribed for by an eligible Investor may be reallocated among the other eligible Investors. Such right of first refusal will terminate upon a Qualified IPO.

Purchase Agreement: The investment shall be made pursuant to a Stock Purchase Agreement reasonably acceptable to the Company and the Investors, which agreement shall contain, among other things, appropriate representations and warranties of the Company, covenants of the Company reflecting the provisions set forth herein and appropriate conditions of closing, including a management rights letter and an opinion of counsel for the Company.

EMPLOYEE MATTERS

Employee Pool: Prior to the Closing, the Company will reserve 977,142 shares of its Common Stock (approximately 12.5% of its fully diluted capital stock following the issuance of its Series A Preferred) for issuances to directors, officers, employees and consultants ("Employee Pool"). As of the date of this financing no options are issued.

Stock Vesting: All stock and stock equivalents issued after the Closing to employees, directors, consultants and other service providers will be subject to vesting as follows (unless different vesting is approved by the unanimous consent of the Board of Directors): 25% to vest at the end of the first year following such issuance, with the remaining 75% to vest monthly over the next three years. The repurchase option shall provide that upon termination of the employment of the stockholder, with or without cause, the Company or its assignee (to the extent permissible under applicable securities law qualification) retains the option to repurchase at cost any vested shares held by such stockholder. Any issuance of shares in excess of the Employee Pool not approved by the Board will be a dilutive event requiring adjustment of the conversion price as provided above and will be subject to the Investors' first offer right as described above. The two founders' shares will vest as follows: 25% to vest at the end of the first year following such issuance, with the remaining 75% to vest yearly over the next five years.

Restrictions on Sales: The Company's Bylaws shall contain a right of first refusal on all transfers of Common Stock, subject to normal exceptions. If the Company elects not to exercise its right, the Company shall assign its right to the Investors on a pro-rata basis.

Proprietary Information
and
Inventions Agreement: Each current and former officer, employee and consultant of the Company shall enter into an acceptable proprietary information and inventions agreement.

Co-Sale Agreement: The shares of the Company's securities held by the Founders and certain other key employees shall be made subject to a co-sale agreement (with certain reasonable exceptions) with the Investors such that the Founders may not sell, transfer or exchange their stock unless each Investor has an opportunity to participate in the sale on a pro-rata basis. This right of co-sale shall not apply to and shall terminate upon a Qualified IPO.

OTHER MATTERS

Assignment: Each of the Investors shall be entitled to transfer all or part of its shares of Series A Preferred purchased by it to one or more affiliated partnerships or funds managed by it or any of their respective directors, officers or partners, provided such transferee agrees in writing to be subject to the terms of the Stock Purchase Agreement and related agreements as if it were a purchaser there under.

Indemnification: The Company will indemnify board members to the broadest extent permitted by applicable law and will indemnify each investor for any claims brought against the investors by any third party (including any other stockholder of the Company) as a result of this financing.

Conditions Precedent
to Financing: This summary of terms is not intended as a legally binding commitment by the Investors, and any obligation on the part of the Investors is subject to the following conditions precedent:

1. Completion of legal documentation satisfactory to the prospective Investors.

2. Satisfactory completion of due diligence by the prospective Investors.

Finders:	The Company and the Investors shall each indemnify the other for any broker's or finder's fees for which either is responsible.
Investor Counsel:	Smith & Hutch
Legal Fees and Expenses:	The Company shall bear its own fees and expenses and shall pay the reasonable fees (not to exceed $5,000) for investors counsel. The company shall bear Investors' out of pocket due diligence advisory expenses.

Acknowledged and agreed:

Eagle Ventures

By:_____

Print Name:_____

Title: _____

Lime Tree, Inc.

By:_____

Print Name:_____

Title: _____

Glossary

Accredited investor: In certain situations, such as when making investments in risky new ventures, the U.S. Securities and Exchange Commission (SEC) limits the sale of stock/equity to those who are deemed sophisticated in financial matters or who appear better able to afford a loss. These individuals are referred to as accredited investors. As of 2007, the SEC's definition of an individual accredited investor is a person whose individual net worth, or joint net worth with a spouse, is in excess of $1 million, or one whose income has exceeded $200,000 in the past two years or whose joint income with a spouse was more than $300,000 in the past two years—and who has a reasonable expectation of reaching the same income level in the current year.

Anti-dilution provisions: Provisions in the **Stock Purchase Agreement** that enable an investor to maintain the value of the shares of their stock in subsequent **financing rounds**—in other words, to prevent the value of their shares from being diluted. Typically, these provisions give investors the right to receive additional shares, without cost, if shares are sold in subsequent rounds at lower prices than they originally paid, in an amount that would maintain the value of their investment. Other anti-dilution provisions guarantee investors the right to purchase additional shares of stock in future funding rounds to maintain their same percentage level of ownership.

Bootstrapping: Growing a business through sales and income rather than through funding from outside investors. Bootstrapping could include conventional financing, such as bank loans.

Capitalization table (also called "cap table"): A list detailing the total amount of stock/securities issued by a company and how much was paid for that stock. Typically, this includes the amount of investment obtained from each source, the number of shares of stock received in return for each investment, the per share purchase price, and the types of securities involved—such as common or preferred shares, options, convertible notes, or warrants. A capitalization table gives a quick snapshot of the total ownership and equity of a company.

Common stock: Stock (in other words, **securities**) representing shares of ownership of a company—with normal rights that are enjoyed by all owners of that type of stock. In this regard, common stock differs from **preferred stock**, which grants its owners additional rights and privileges.

Convertible preferred stock: **Preferred stock** that can be transformed —or "converted"—into **common stock**. Conversion typically occurs due to an Initial Public Offering (IPO) or other **liquidity event**. Angel investors typically want this kind of stock.

Deal flow: The rate at which investors receive proposals from entrepreneurs seeking financing for their ventures. Angel investors want to increase the quantity and quality of the proposals they see—in other words, to increase their deal flow—so they have the best chance of finding profitable investments.

Dilution: Dilution occurs when the value of an investors' stock is reduced in subsequent rounds of financing because the price of the new shares being sold is lower than the price the investor originally paid. Anti-dilution provisions protect an investor from this. Dilution also occurs when an investor's percentage of ownership in a company is reduced because other investors purchase that company's stock in subsequent funding rounds.

Down round: A financing cycle, or **round**, in which the price per share of stock is lower than the price in a previous round of financing.

Due diligence: The process of investigating the background and credentials of a company, individual, or investor. An angel investor will perform due diligence to make certain that the information an entrepreneur provides, including information in business plans, is accurate.

Entrepreneurs also perform due diligence on potential investors.

Equity: Ownership of part or all of a company. In an angel investment, equity typically is distributed in the form of stock, or shares, of ownership. On a balance sheet, equity (or "shareholder's equity") is the amount of total assets minus total liabilities.

Exit strategy/exit plan (occasionally also known as "harvest strategy"): Potential strategies by which a company can eventually enable investors to recoup the money they have invested. Typical exit strategies include an Initial Public Stock offering (IPO) or acquisition by another company.

Follow-on financing: Subsequent additional investments in a company that will occur after the current financing **round**. Generally, these are larger amounts than in the current funding cycle. Entrepreneurs typically prefer to secure financing from angel investors who are capable of providing follow-on financing themselves or arranging introductions to other investors, such as venture capitalists, who can provide such future financing.

"Hockey stick" growth curve: An exceptionally fast rate of company growth—one that is often preferred by investors. A hockey stick growth curve refers to the line on a financial projections graph that would resemble a hockey stick, with a relatively short development time (the blade of the stick) followed by a steep upward growth in income (the long handle of the stick).

Intellectual property: The intangible assets of a company, specifically those that are the result of knowledge (the product of the mind), rather than physical property. Intellectual property includes assets such as designs, patents, trademarks, copyrights, processes, ideas, and data.

Liquidation preference: Provisions in the **stock purchase agreement** detailing the rights and entitlements of investors in the event that the company fails (is liquidated).

Liquidity event: An occurrence which enables the investor to turn their equity in the company into cash. This event is typically the sale of the company or an Initial Public Offering (IPO) on a stock exchange.

Portfolio: The group of investments (companies) held by an investor, venture capital firm, investment company, or other financing entity.

Portfolio company: One of the companies an angel or venture capital firm has invested in.

Post-money valuation: The total worth or value of a company subsequent to receiving funding in a round of financing. For instance, if a company gives investors 10% of a company for $100,000, the post-money valuation of that company is then $1 million.

Preferred stock: Stock (in other words, **securities**) representing shares of ownership of a company that comes with special rights that are not enjoyed by owners of **common stock**. Some of the privileges granted to holders of preferred stock include the right to receive dividends before common stock holders and, in the event of the liquidation or bankruptcy of the company, to be repaid before common stock holders.

Pre-money valuation: The total worth or value of a company prior to receiving funding in a round of financing.

Restricted stock: When a company goes public on a stock exchange (IPO), limitations are often placed on the sale of stock received or purchased prior to a public offering, especially stock held by people such as angels, company founders, and key employees. These limitations include how much stock can be sold and when. This mechanism is put in place to prevent these early stockholders from suddenly selling all their stock and depressing the stock price, or dumping their stock once there is a public market.

Return on Investment (ROI): The total financial gain an angel investor receives for having put their money in a company. It is expressed in terms of an annual percentage—that is, the percentage of their investment earned each year of the investment (for example, a 30% ROI). This is calculated by dividing the amount of money investors make by the amount they invested, divided by the number of years it took to receive their gains.

Rounds/Financing rounds: A cycle of fundraising for a new business. High-growth businesses typically raise money in several cycles, or rounds, as they grow. A goal is generally set for each round. In any given round, a company may raise funds from a number of investors. Funding rounds are referred to as "Seed," "Series A," "Series B," and so on.

Securities: Stocks, bonds, or other evidence of a holding in a business. Typical securities for an angel-backed business are stocks and stock **warrants**.

Seed stage: The earliest stage of a company's development, typically before it makes sales or ships product.

Stock Purchase Agreement (also known as the "Investment Agreement" or the "Stock Purchase and Sale Agreement"): The Stock Purchase Agreement is the actual contract between entrepreneurs and their investors. It sets forth the specific terms of the purchase and sale of the stock to the investors, such as the purchase price, closing date, conditions to close, and representations and warranties of the parties.

Term Sheet: A non-binding document summarizing all the terms negotiated between an entrepreneur and a potential funder. In effect, it is the offer the angel is making to an entrepreneur. The term sheet will include such items as the agreed-upon **valuation**, the equity the investor will receive, and rights the investor will have.

Valuation: The worth, or value, of a company or other asset. Valuation also refers to the process of determining the worth of a company. Before any money is raised for a new company, its **pre-money valuation** is highly subjective and determined primarily through negotiations among investors and company founders. After raising funds, the **post-money valuation** of a company is more definite.

Vesting: The right to receive something at a future date. In angel investments, vesting generally refers to stock or stock options granted to individuals, such as company founders or key employees, that will be earned over a period of time. Angel investors negotiate vesting schedules with entrepreneurs to ensure that key employees will remain with the company.

Warrant: A right to purchase additional shares of stock (either **common** or **preferred**) at a specified price over a defined period of time. Investors, key employees, and others may receive stock warrants, and when exercised, such warrants can dilute the ownership interest of other stockholders.

Index

Acknowledgments

Rhonda Abrams would like to thank:

Maggie Canon, Managing Editor. Maggie brings an outstanding background in the publishing industry to her position with The Planning Shop. She was founding editor of *InfoWorld* and numerous other technology magazines and was also managing editor of the bestselling *America 24/7* series. Maggie's energy, professionalism, and intelligence have been invaluable additions to The Planning Shop.

Mireille Majoor, Editorial Project Manager, who oversees the editorial process of this and every Planning Shop book. She is a consummate professional and both The Planning Shop's books and readers have benefited from Mireille's commitment to excellence.

Deborah Kaye, who manages The Planning Shop's relations with the academic community. Deborah's unwavering dedication to the professors and students who use our books and resources has earned her a large group of devoted academic fans. Deborah has been The Planning Shop's guiding light for many years and we are continually appreciative of her contribution.

Rosa Whitten, Office Manager and the newest member of The Planning Shop's team. Rosa comes to us with years of organizational experience. She is already proving to be invaluable—in terms of both her skills and her positive outlook. We are delighted to have her help to guide us.

Arthur Wait, who designed the look and feel of The Planning Shop's line of books and products and developed our website and electronic products. We are always amazed (though no longer surprised) by the range of Arthur's talents.

Diana Van Winkle, who brought her graphic expertise to the design of this book. She is talented, responsive, and a delight to work with. Diana's skills ensure that The Planning Shop's books continue to be easy and pleasurable for readers to use.

Kathryn Dean, who brought her eagle eye to the copyediting and proofing process, ensuring that our books are pristine and error free.

Tracey Taylor would like to thank the following people for their expertise on a range of topics relating to angel investing:

Larry Fenster, independent angel investor, Denver, Colorado; Laura Hill, Educational Program Coordinator, University of New Hampshire, Center for Venture Research; Marianne Hudson, Director, Angel Initiatives, Ewing Marion Kauffman Foundation; Guy Kawasaki, Managing Director, Garage Technology Ventures; Lance Knobel, Editor-in-Chief, Q Network Inc; Mark Leiter, Chairman, Leiter & Company and member of the New York Angels; Jim Parrish, Certified Business Analyst, Florida's Small Business Development Center; Laura Roden, Managing Director, The Angels' Forum; Professor Jeffrey E. Sohl, University of New Hampshire, Center for Venture Research; Jeff Stinson, Executive Director, Fund for Arkansas' Future; John S. Taylor, Vice President of Research, National Venture Capital Association.

Notes:

Notes:

Notes:

There's more where this book came from!

Ask your bookseller about these other In A Day titles from The Planning Shop, or buy direct at:
www.PlanningShop.com

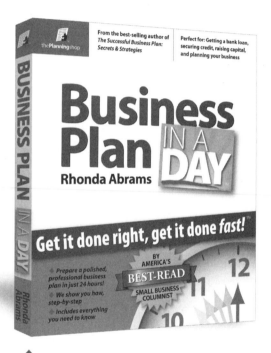

When you've got to wow an audience—whether it's making a persuasive sales presentation to a key customer, an internal report to senior management, or a motivational keynote to a packed auditorium— this book will help you get prepped, pumped, and ready to go—fast.

"Let me take a look at your business plan." If you've heard these words from a potential lender, investor or business partner, and you need a plan fast, this book is for you. The step-by-step guide delivers the critical, time-tested information and tools you need to develop a winning plan— quickly and efficiently.

Finish your plan's financial projections *faster!*

The Planning Shop's Electronic Financial Worksheets streamline the time-consuming, tedious process of creating and formatting financial statements.

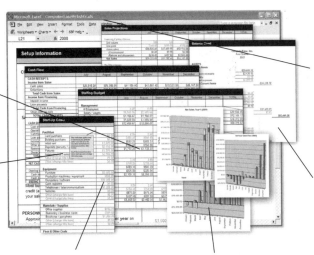

All the math and calculations are done for you!

"Help Balloons" provide convenient information and advice and refer you to the relevant pages in the book for further information.

Built on Microsoft Excel, the powerful industry standard for generating compelling financial reports.

When you're finished, just print out your Income Statement, Cash-Flow Projections, and Balance Sheets and add them to your plan!

Fill out the information in one worksheet and it automatically transfers to other appropriate worksheets.

Charts and graphs are automatically generated for you!

Create financials on your computer!
The Planning Shop has developed this Excel-based package of worksheets and financial statements to work hand-in-hand with *The Successful Business Plan* and *Business Plan In A Day*.

"Flow-Through Financials" Save Time!
Enter your financial figures just once, and they'll automatically flow-through to all the other relevant statements—necessary calculations will be performed along the way! Don't create your financials from scratch—let us do the work for you!

Download your copy today at our lowest price:
www.PlanningShop.com

Grow Your Business with The Planning Shop!

We offer a full complement of books and tools to help you build your business **successfully**.

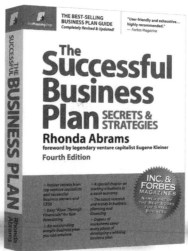

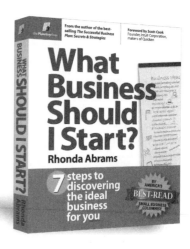

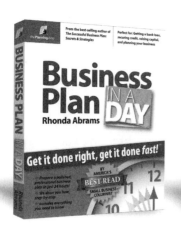

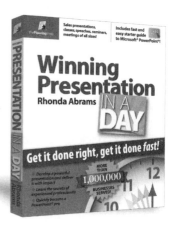

Ask your bookseller about these titles
or visit www.PlanningShop.com